THE
Quotable
BILLY
GRAHAM

Compiled and Edited
by CORT R. FLINT
and the Staff of *Quote*

DROKE HOUSE
Publishers
ANDERSON, S. C.

Library of Congress Catalog Card Number: 66–25566

Published By DROKE HOUSE, Publishers,
309 S. Main, Anderson, S. C.

MANUFACTURED IN THE UNITED STATES OF AMERICA
FOR DROKE HOUSE, PUBLISHERS
BY
KINGSPORT PRESS, INC., KINGSPORT, TENN.
DESIGNED BY W. J. MC INTOSH

THE
Quotable
BILLY
GRAHAM

Contents

Introduction

Tens of millions of people have heard Billy Graham preach personally. Hundreds of millions have seen him on television or heard him on the radio. His books have sold millions of copies. He is one of the most widely known men in the world today.

And yet no one volume has been available to the divinity student, the minister, or those whose lives have been changed by this greatest of all evangelists, in which could be found what Billy Graham said or thought or had written on all subjects.

A reference book was needed to present the "complete" Billy Graham—a book to aid, to give ideas and understanding, to bring the reader closer to God. This is what I have tried to do in compiling and editing THE QUOTABLE BILLY GRAHAM.

I first knew Billy Graham when he was beginning his career as a young evangelist. I realized even then that he had God's hands on him in a very unique way. As president of the Pastors Conference in Louisville, Kentucky, and Administrative Assistant at the Southern Baptist Theological Seminary, I talked with the Seminary's President Duke K. McCall, who has always been deeply concerned with evangelism. He, too, felt that God planned a place of leadership for Billy Graham, and we were determined to do everything we could to give him assurance, and to help open doors for his ministry. We enlisted the aid of the trustees, faculty, staff, and student body of the seminary as well as the pastors; and Billy was invited there for a Mission and Evangelistic Emphasis Day.

This initial visit led to the establishment of the Billy Graham Room in the Seminary's Library, to keep a permanent record of his evangelistic ministry; and a Billy Graham Chair of Evangelism, which I, as first Vice-chairman of the trustees, had a part in establishing.

Throughout the years I have participated in as many of Billy Graham's crusades as possible and have had the privilege to call him my friend.

It has been a great joy and an honor to edit the quotations of a man whom I respect and admire.

CORT R. FLINT

Billy Graham, beyond any minister of Christ in the world, speaks to this generation. What he has to say is pertinent to every man in every nation on the face of the globe. Billy Graham has a message from God and what he says is filled with godly admonition for our souls. A record of what this world-famed evangelist has spoken under the inspiration of the Holy Spirit should be a part of the possession of every family on earth.

> Dr. W. A. Criswell
> Pastor
> First Baptist Church
> Dallas, Texas
> Of which Billy Graham is a member.

Acknowledgments

The Publishers acknowledge, with deep appreciation, the cooperation of Dr. Billy Graham in granting permission to print in this volume excerpts from his copyrighted works, spoken and written. A debt of gratitude is also due The Crusade Team and The Billy Graham Evangelistic Association for their cooperation in making the compilation of this book possible.

The previously unpublished quotations in this book were obtained by the editor, Cort R. Flint, directly from Billy Graham, from the files of The Billy Graham Evangelistic Association or from The Billy Graham Room, Southern Baptist Theological Seminary, Louisville, Ky.

The Publishers also wish to express appreciation to Dr. Flint for his tireless effort in compiling and editing this book, along with Robert T. Owens, Executive Editor, and the entire editorial staff of *Quote Magazine*.

WILTON HALL, JR.
Publisher
DROKE HOUSE
1966

13

QUOTATIONS

· · A · ·

ACTION

...**Faith.** Our faith grows by expression. If we want to keep our faith, we must share it. We must act.   [1

...**Faith; Commitment.** Faith becomes action, and the action is faith as commitment.   [2

ADOPTION

Roy Rogers and Dale Evans have adopted several children. Once I asked them if they gave the same rights and privileges to their adopted children as they gave to their real children. They were shocked and said: "Of course, we do. They are ours as much as the ones who were born to us. They have all the rights and privileges of our own flesh and blood." We, too, have been adopted into the family of God, with all the rights and privileges of sonship.   [3

ADULTERY

Real marriage, which is the foundation of the home, means the total commitment of husband and wife to each other and does not permit extra-marital adultery or any form of infidelity.   [4

AFRICA

What happens in Africa is going to affect every American. Christianity has done more to awaken Africa than any other ideology . . . but there are others battling for the soul and mind of it. If it should turn to one of the others, Africa would be plunged into a chaos such as we have not experienced in modern history.   [5

. . . Christian Missions.   In Africa alone 85 per cent of all education south of the Sahara has been done by Christian missions. Christian missions around the world have built hospitals and schools and institutions to help people; it is under the impact of Christianity that many of the social problems of the world have been reduced and conditions improved.   [6

. . . Gospel.   It was God's purpose to send the Gospel south into Africa, below the Sahara Desert. That is why He brought Philip from a great evangelistic campaign to deal with the Ethiopian. He was opening up a whole continent through one man. And when missionaries arrived in Africa centuries later, they found the Christian church in Ethiopia and Christian groups elsewhere on the continent, all because of the Gospel that was brought originally by this great nobleman who was led to Christ by Philip.   [7

AGE

. . . Old.   The neglect of older people is becoming an increasing sin in America.   [8

ALCOHOL

...Americans. Most Americans are indifferent concerning the problem of excessive drinking. They hark back to the days when people cried, "Prohibition causes drinking!" But they do not seem to be aware that legalized liquor has brought even more drinking. The simple truth is—man is the same under either system, and if we don't find something to fill his empty heart, he will stuff his stomach with artificial stimulants.   [9

...Crime. Our crime rate has increased in exact ratio to our consumption of alcoholic beverages.   [10

...Drinking. A man may not be responsible for his last drink, but he certainly was for the first.   [11

...Sin. Drinking was a sin first and a disease later.   [12

ALCOHOLICS

Alcoholics are being produced in the United States at the rate of more than twelve hundred a day—over fifty an hour —around the clock.   [13

It poses a major problem for police, sociologists, and ministers of the gospel. So grave is the problem that many of them are unable to cope with the rising tide of drunkenness and its side effects on the populace.   [14

AMBITION

Ambition is an essential part of character, but it must be fixed on lawful objects and exercised in proper proportion.   [15

AMERICA

Whether we know it or not, we are becoming more and more a secularistic nation, where man himself is becoming an idol. We are humanizing God and deifying man.   [16

...**Awakening.**   One of the healthiest and most promising signs on the national horizon is the realization of spiritual and moral need that is sweeping this nation. Many of our most cynical leaders are now admitting that America needs a religious and moral bath that will cleanse it from deception, immorality and lethargy.   [17

...**Church.**   You take the church out of America, and see what kind of hell you'd have here overnight. [18

...**Declaration Of Independence.**   The ethical and moral concepts of Christianity are found all the way through the Declaration of Independence. It was on July 4, 1776, that fifty men gathered in Independence Hall in Philadelphia to declare this nation free from Great Britain and they affixed their signatures and then the Liberty Bell rang out. It was the birthday of a small nation that was to become the mightiest and greatest nation the world has ever known. Down through the years God has mightily blessed America.   [19

...**False Gods.**   This is a picture of America today: worshiping other gods while giving lip service to the true and the living God.   [20

...**Peril.**   From the beginning of the Bible to the end, God warns that any nation which departs from Him is going to suffer judgment. America has been given more spiritual and moral light than any nation in the history of the world, and yet this great nation has departed from Him and stands in peril of His judgment. [21

AMERICANS

My travels around the world have shown me that Americans live in a fish-bowl with the whole world looking in. [22

...Emptiness. America is said to have the highest per capita boredom of any spot on earth! We know that because we have the greatest variety and greatest number of artificial amusements of any country. People have become so empty that they can't even entertain themselves. They have to pay other people to amuse them, to make them laugh, to try to make them feel warm and happy and comfortable for a few minutes, to try to lose that awful, frightening, hollow feeling —that terrible, dreaded feeling of being lost and alone. [23

...Heritage. The early Americans were angry, disturbed, articulate people. They were angry at tyranny, prejudice, intolerance and injustice, and angry enough to talk about it and do something about it. It was not the fearful and the soft who made this country, but the articulate and the courageous men who changed this wilderness into the mighty nation that it is today. [24

...Russians. Americans are no special pets in the eyes of God. He loves the Russians just as much. [25

...Speaking Out. The hypocrites, the fakers, the phonies, the bigots and the extremists are all talking. Few people are more articulate than they. Now it is time for the little, everyday people to speak out when they really believe something is right. [26

ANGER

Anger is a heinous sin because it reveals the animal nature of man. [27

Anger breeds remorse in the heart, discord in the home, bitterness in the community and confusion in the state. [28

... **Control.** When a man gives way to anger and loses control of his tongue, he is committing sin. [29

... **Murder.** Anger is the parent of murder. [30

... **Varieties.** Anger has many varieties—indignation, irritation, impatience, vexation, bitterness, exasperation, resentment, passion, temper, wrath, rage, pouting, carrying a grudge—and these are expressed in all sorts of ill-tempered words ranging from the cold acid of sarcasm to the hot flame of fury. [31

ANXIETY

Modern anxiety is not directed toward the real, valid, justified fears such as eternity, death, and the judgment of God. This generation is dying, not from external pressure, but from internal combustion. [32

Historians will probably call our era "the age of anxiety." Though we have less to worry about than previous generations, we have more worry. [33

The anxieties and burdens of life rest so heavily upon men and women because their souls cry out for God and never find rest. [34

...**Cause.** Anxiety is the natural result when our hopes are centered in anything short of God and His will for us. [35

...**Cure.** To all who wish to be rid of anxiety, I would make three simple suggestions: First, stop seeking the trivial, transient things with which modern man has become surfeited, and seek the Kingdom of God as it is revealed in Christ. Second, get your eyes off yourself; focus them upon God first and others second. Third, commit yourself fully to Christ. [36

APATHY

History shows that when a people cease to care enough to fight for their freedom, their society is on its way to oblivion. When they lose the ability to take a risk, and the will to accept the challenge to make their communities safe and free, they cannot long endure. [37

ARROGANCE

...**Misery.** Arrogance has its own built-in misery. The arrogant person may offend others, but he hurts himself more. [38

ASSURANCE

...**Faith.** Many people completely lack assurance because they have failed to understand a very necessary truth of the Christian experience: Faith brings assurance![39

ATHEISM

. . . Christian. I think that it is a contradiction to say that there is such a thing as Christian atheism. [40

. . . Freud. Sigmund Freud attacked the idea of God in a little book called, "The Future of an Illusion." He said, "When man is freed of religion, he has a better chance to live a normal and wholesome life." [41

. . . Karl Marx. Karl Marx was another who sought to deny the existence of God. He said, "The idea of God is the keystone of a perverted society. It must be destroyed. The true root of liberty, equality and culture is atheism." [42

. . . Result. If you say there is no God, then lying, murder, anything you want to do, is permitted. [43

ATOMIC AGE

On July 16, 1945, a light brighter than a thousand suns illuminated the desert sands of New Mexico. One scientist who was watching wept aloud: "My God, we have created hell." From that day on our world has not been the same. We entered a new era of history—perhaps the last era. [44

ATONEMENT

William Tyndale, who translated the New Testament into English, encountered difficulty in finding a word to convey the meaning of Christ's redeeming work. Finding no suitable word, he joined two simple words—"at" and "one-ment," making "atonement" and giving, in its etymology, a clue to the Bible's teaching of salvation by reconciliation.[45

AUTOMOBILE SAFETY

We say that the slaughter in Viet Nam has been terrible but we lose more people in one month on the highways of America than the total Viet Nam War has cost us. So it's far safer to be fighting in Viet Nam than driving on the highways. Did you know that one of every two Americans will be in an automobile wreck before he dies? One out of every two. And we smile at it, and laugh at it—at death, death, death on the highways. [46

... **Drivers.** We've heard that cars and roads are not safe —but you hear very little discussion of the driver. The great problem is the driver: the man who drinks and gets in the car, the man who gets mad at his wife and goes out on the highway and takes it out on the people he's driving with. I think we need a great program teaching that highway safety is basically a moral and spiritual problem. [47

AVARICE

Avarice is as much a part of the natural man as breathing. [48

Avarice, the close relative of covetousness, is probably the parent of more evil than all the other sins. [49

... **Judas.** Driven by avarice, Judas sold his Lord for thirty pieces of silver, but found out that life was not worth living without Him. [50

AWARENESS

What a tragedy it is for people to mourn the loss of material things, which they will lose anyway, and to be totally unconcerned about spiritual things, which are eternal. [51

·· B ··

BEHAVIOR

... **Destruction.** Psychologists tell us the seed of murder lurks in the heart of the most respected person. But only those who kill the body are punishable by the law, while many who are abroad are just as guilty of destroying the lives, the personalities, and the souls of those near and dear to them. [52

BELIEF

... **Action.** Unless our belief in God causes us to help our fellowman, our faith stands condemned. Our love for God is best proved by our regard for the needs of our neighbors. [53

When we speak of Christian faith, we refer to certain beliefs and doctrines. These are of great importance, for Christian living presupposes Christian conviction. But it is possible to have beliefs which do not find expression in conduct. This belief of the head is often confused with real faith. The simple truth is: one really believes only that which he acts upon. [54

... **Commitment.** A man of any race, a man of any nationality, a man of any language can believe, and that's all God says you have to do to get to heaven—just believe. Now that word "believe" may be a little more than you think it is. It means commitment; it means surrender; it means that I give everything that I have to Jesus Christ and trust Him alone for my forgiveness and my salvation. [55

... **Definition.** Leighton Ford has said: "Belief is not faith without evidence but commitment without reservation." [56

BIBLE

... **Approach To.** We should approach the Bible with the assurance that here we have God-breathed literature; that it is our privilege and joy to find out what He has to say. [57

... **Authority.** The only real authority we have is God's Word, the Bible. His Word sheds light on human nature, world problems and human suffering. But beyond that it delineates and reveals the way back to God. [58

... **Christianity.** True Christianity finds all of its doctrines in the Bible; true Christianity does not deny any part of the Bible; true Christianity does not add anything to the Bible. [59

... **Constitution.** The Bible is the constitution of Christianity. Just as the United States Constitution is not of any private interpretation, neither is the Bible of any private interpretation. Just as the Constitution includes all who live under its stated domain, without exception, so the Bible includes all who live under its stated domain, without exception. [60

...Nature; Conscience. Nature in her laws tells of God, but the message is not too clear. It tells us nothing of the love and grace of God. Conscience, in our inmost being, does tell us of God, but the message is fragmentary. The only place we can find a clear, unmistakable message is in the Word of God, which we call the Bible. [61

...Prophecy. The Bible accurately predicted Christ's first advent in every detail. Hundreds of years before Jesus was born, the Bible revealed that He would be of the tribe of Judah, that He would be born in Bethlehem, that He would be born of a virgin, that He would flee into Egypt, that He would heal the sick, that His own people would reject Him, that He would be betrayed by a friend and sold for 30 pieces of silver, that He would be crucified with sinners, that His side would be pierced, that He would be raised from the dead and that He would ascend into heaven. [62

...Prophesying. The Bible teaches that God has a plan and it's the only book in the world that looks into the future. The Bible is the only sacred book in the world that even claims to look into the future and tell us exactly what is going to happen. [63

...Reading. You would not expect to lead a healthy physical life unless you ate your meals regularly. Show the same amount of common sense about building up your spiritual life into a healthy, vigorous state. Daily Bible reading is essential to victorious living and real Christian growth. [64

... **Sin.** The Bible tells you that man has a spiritual disease called sin. This book tells you the cure. The cure is Jesus Christ. But if you reject God's diagnosis of the human disease and reject the cure, then there's no hope, so you grow in your blindness. [65

... **Temptation.** The Bible is the only thing that can combat the devil. Quote the Scriptures and the devil will run . . . use the Scriptures like a sword and you'll drive temptation away. [66

... **Value.** The Bible, the greatest document of the human race, remains a bulwark of national, personal and spiritual freedom. [67

BIRTH
... **Death.** The Bible says there is a time to be born and a time to die. Birth is a happy event. Death is a tragic event and we have tears. [68

BIRTH CONTROL
I am in favor of birth control to stop the population explosion. [69

... **America.** A Great Society needs some form of birth control. [70

...**Population Explosion.** The world in the light of increasing population will be one great city unless something is done to control population. [71

BODY

...**Soul.** We cannot be dedicated to Christ without giving Him our bodies. The devil gets at the soul through the body. Take your body—your hands, your feet, all of you —and present it to Christ. [72

...**Spirit.** Spirit is contrary to body. Spirit is opposite to body. Spirit is something that is not limited by a body. Spirit is not bound in a body. Spirit is not wearable as a body. Spirit is not changeable as a body. [73

BOREDOM

Thousands are bored with life because they lack a knowledge of its real meaning. [74

...**Creativity.** No one is bored who is creative. Only those who want to have everything done for them are bored. [75

...**Man.** The only one of God's creatures who is capable of being bored is man. [76

...**Modern Life.** Modern living, with its gadgets flowing from the production line, has created a new disease called boredom. [77

BREVITY

During a Crusade (1957) I asked a congressman to address the congregation "briefly." He said: "That's a most unscriptural injunction, Billy. Remember, the Bible says, 'Thou shalt not muzzle the ox that treadeth out the corn.'" [78

BROKEN HOMES

Almost every historian will agree that the disintegration of the Roman Empire was due largely to the broken home. In a recent study of moral conditions in Greece, Persia, and Babylonia, the scholars agreed that divorces and broken homes, more than any other single factor, contributed to the downfall of these nations. [79

... **Reasons.** Hundreds of persons write that their homes have been broken because of excessive drinking. Hundreds of others confess that unfaithfulness on the part of the husband or wife is responsible. Others mention jealousy, maladjustment, selfishness, the craving for pleasure, as contributing factors. [80

BROTHERHOOD

We will never build a brotherhood of man upon earth until we are all brothers in Christ Jesus. [81

BUDDHA

I think Buddha was a great man, but at the end of Buddha's life, he said, "I'm still searching for the truth." Christ said, "I am the truth." [82

··C··

CAIN

Cain is the original architect of our modern civilization. He is the self-sufficient materialist, the religious humanist.   [83

CALVARY

...Decision. Calvary is the place of decision. It is the eternal sword, erected to divide men into two classes, the saved and the lost. Embrace its truth and be saved. Reject it and be lost.   [84

...Love. The world had never seen such a manifestation of selfless love as was demonstrated upon Calvary. [85

...Sin. If your sins are not responsible for Calvary, then Calvary has no responsibility for your sins.   [86

CENSORSHIP

...Pornography. Strict censorship is the best answer to the problems of pornography. Either this, or the morals of our youth will be gravely endangered.   [87

CHEATING

They say that 75% of all college students cheat sometime or other during their college careers. But God demands honesty and integrity wherever you are, whatever you are doing. This includes your efforts while in high school, college or business life. Cheating will rob you of any right relationship with God.   [88

... **Athletics; Golf.** Of all games, golf is supposed to be a game of honor. It is a game for gentlemen, and if the rules are not observed it ceases to be any fun for anyone. In fact, it ceases to be golf. When anyone wants to win so badly that he resorts to cheating, he is missing the whole point of the game. If he wins he has really lost, for he has lost that feeling of honor and good sportsmanship that is the point of every fair athletic contest.   [89

... **School.** I have found that if a young person cheats in school he has a tendency to cheat in life. It starts a trend and he begins to harden his heart and this becomes a terrible danger.   [90

CHILDREN

... **Church.** Children need a spiritual example set in the home. All too often parents take their children to Sunday School but never set the example by going themselves. One of the greatest insurances against juvenile delinquency is faithful church attendance.   [91

... **Insecurity.** Children are not so much upset by physical insecurity as they are by emotional upheavals, or the lack of love. During World War II, when Britain was being bombed nightly, many British parents sent their children to the country where they could be safe from the bombings. But social studies made after the war showed that the children who stayed in London with their parents, where, despite the bombings, they could have the security of love and understanding, were less disturbed than those who were isolated from home in areas of comparative safety. [92

... **Juvenile Delinquency.** Six suggestions on how to curb juvenile delinquency: 1–Take time with your children; 2–Set your children a good example; 3–Give your children ideals for living; 4–Have a lot of activities planned for your children; 5–Discipline your children; 6–Teach them about God. [93

... **Obedience; Discipline.** We are living in a day when many psychiatrists are saying that the child should be allowed to express himself freely and to do as he pleases. But the Bible teaches that there should be loving obedience on the part of the child, and that if he does not obey, then discipline should be exercised by the parents. [94

... **Obedience To Parents.** The parent who does not teach his child to obey is being cruel to him. The habit of implicit obedience to parental authority is the foundation of good citizenship. More than that, it is the foundation of subjection to God's authority. [95

... **Parental Authority.** Parents do wrong by failing to exercise wise and loving authority over their children Children are born with an innate instability and with a desire to be directed and guided. If they discover that their parents are weak instead of strong, and incapable of leading them properly, their personalities are affected. They will then seek and find unwholesome and improper leadership in hoodlum gangs, terror clubs and sadistic rings.   [96

... **Parents; Counseling.** A child needs wise and prayerful counseling on the part of parents. Many children are afraid to go to their parents for counsel. Parents many times treat children as children when they often need to be talked to like grownups.   [97

... **Respect.** Children who are allowed to be disrespectful to their parents will not have any true respect for anyone.   [98

... **Spoiling.** Coddling children, sparing them from correction, is one of the primary causes of delinquency.   [99

... **Understanding.** A child needs understanding. Many parents do not try to reason with their children, they do not try to understand them.   [100

CHRIST

The Bible predicts that some day a man from outer space will arrive on this planet. That man is Christ.   [101

... **Acceptance.** You are not born again when you die. The great change is not death. The great change is when you come to Christ. For then you become a partaker of God's life.   [102

36

...Blood Of. The blood of Christ may seem to be a grim, repulsive subject to those who do not realize its true significance, but to those who have accepted His redemption and have been set free from sin's chains, the blood of Christ is precious. The freed slave never forgets the overwhelming cost of his liberty and freedom.   [103

...Church. People in various church organizations are calling for us to look for the "church within the church." Some are even saying that the greatest problem Christianity faces is the "walls of the church." Can we get through the church to find Jesus Himself? If we can, we will find that He Himself, and not any single group, is the answer.[104

...Coming. Christ made it clear that His coming, far from meaning peace, meant war. His message was a fire that would set society ablaze with division and strife. [105

...His Message. Christ's message was revolutionizing; His words simple, yet profound. And His words provoked either happy acceptance or violent rejection. Men were never the same after listening to Him.   [106

...How To Receive Him. First: recognize that God loved you so much that He gave His Son to die on the cross. Second: repent of your sins. Third: receive Jesus Christ as Savior and Lord. Fourth: confess Christ publicly.   [107

...Injustice; Prejudice. Christ taught that His fire would eventually destroy the bonds of fear, ignorance, in-

justice and racial prejudice. But He also warned that this
will mean division and strife.   [108

...Perfection. There are people who have emphasized
Christ's deity over His humanity, to the point that some
forget that He *was* human. There are others who are empha-
sizing His humanity and deny His deity. He was both—God
and man. He was: "The God-man." He was the man that
God meant all men to be. He was the absolute perfect man
in every respect.   [109

...Power. The moment you receive Christ, He not only
forgives your sin but the Holy Spirit comes to dwell inside of
you, to give you a supernatural power to live a new life.[110

If you decide to live for Jesus Christ and go all out for
Him, He'll be in your heart and He'll be there when every
moral choice is made to help you over the humps and problems and difficulties and temptations. He'll give you a new
power and new strength to resist temptation.   [111

...Sin, Cure For. There is only one specific curative for
the disease of sin and that is the atoning blood of Jesus
Christ. Many elect to reject the only true remedy and resort
to synthetics and substitutes, but none of these will effect a
cure.   [112

...Truth. When a man writes a question mark over
what Christ has said, it is a means of dodging the truth rather
than an honest attempt to discover it.   [113

...Victorious. Since a living Christ dwells within every one of us who has accepted Him as Savior, there is never any reason for defeat. No enemy is too powerful for Christ.[114

CHRISTIAN

...Discipline. It has been observed that children can steal before they can walk, and lie before they can talk; so religious training and Christian discipline cannot begin too soon.   [115

...Education. You do not become a Christian as the result of a process of education, but rather through redemption and faith.   [116

...Holy Life; Example. An atheist once spent a few days with Fenelon and said, "If I stay with this man of God much longer, I shall become a Christian in spite of myself." The quiet, convincing argument of a holy life, and the consistent walk of the saint, Fenelon, had accomplished more in the life of an atheist than all of the theological arguments and discussions he had ever heard.   [117

...Strength. If you are not strengthening the inner man by daily walking with God now, when a crisis comes you will quake with fear, and give in, having no strength to stand up for Christ.   [118

CHRISTIANITY

...Applied. We have not practiced applied Christianity. We have restricted it to a Sunday affair.   [119

... Caricature. One of the great problems we face today is the caricature of Christianity that is carried in the minds of modern men. They see our great edifices, but do they see the dynamic life that Jesus Christ promised to all who have a personal encounter with Him? [120

... Definition. Christianity isn't only going to church on Sunday. It is living 24 hours of every day with Jesus Christ. [121

... Exclusivity. Christianity is an exclusive rather than an inclusive ideology. It is broad in its embrace but narrow in its demands and requirements. [122

... Satisfaction. Suppose someone should offer me a plateful of crumbs after I had eaten a T-bone steak. I would say, "No, thank you. I am already satisfied." Christian, that is the secret—you can be so filled with the things of Christ, so enamored with the things of God that you do not have time for the sinful pleasures of this world. [123

... Victory. A Christianity which knows no victory over sin is no better than heathenism which knows no victory over sin. [124

CHRISTIAN LIFE

... Conflict. The Bible indicates that the Christian life is a life of conflict and warfare. [125

... Difficulty. Following Christ is a hard, rugged life. There is nothing easy or sissy about it. [126

. . . Power Of. Are we Christians going to talk of all the power of Jesus, yet never really have that power in sufficient quantity to bring a great spiritual revival?   [127

. . . Realities. The Bible teaches that with Christ in your heart you can face the realities of life, and even though they are hard, the grace of God will give you greater joy and pleasure than any dream-world to which you may try to escape.   [128

. . . Worldly Life. The life lived for what this world offers seems futile and empty, tawdry and trivial compared with the utter satisfaction, the glorious joys and lasting pleasures which a person finds in Christ and in the Christian life.   [129

CHRISTIANS

. . . Action. The New Testament seems to indicate that the real test is not only in creeds but in deeds. "By their fruits ye shall know them."   [130

. . . Business. It is not easy to be a Christian in our complex business world.   [131

. . . Example. The Christian should stand out like a sparkling diamond against a rough background.   [132

. . . Life. The Christian must live his life in this world. He must infiltrate this world with a purpose—to help win the world.   [133

... **Modern Life.** Nowhere in the New Testament do I find that Christians are to expect to be popular, comfortable and successful in the eyes of this age. [134

... **Mothers.** We need Christian mothers more than we need atomic bombs and new planes. [135

... **Pleasure.** We must always distinguish between wholesome, God-ordained pleasure and sinful, wordly pleasure. Christians have more wholesome fun than anyone in the world, but their joy wells up from within. [136

... **Prohibitions.** Some of the most unattractive Christians in the world are those who have built a fence of prohibitions around themselves and keep most people outside the fence. [137

... **Sincerity.** Don't be a half-Christian. There are too many of them in the world already. The world has a profound respect for a man who is sincere in his faith. [138

... **Worldliness.** Sometimes it becomes difficult to tell a Christian from a worldling. [139

Too many Christians have geared their program to please, entertain and gain the favor of this world. We are concerned with how much, instead of how little, like this age we can become. [140

CHRISTMAS

On that first Christmas night in Bethlehem, "God was manifest in the flesh" (1 Timothy 3:16). This manifestation was in the person of Jesus Christ. [141

Christmas time is a time of joy, but we must make sure that it is not pagan joy generated by the expectation of receiving gifts or engaging in revelry. The real happiness of Christmas is in the fact of the Incarnation, that God was in Christ, reconciling the world unto Himself. [142

Christmas is not a myth, not a tradition, not a dream—it is a glorious reality. For from that manger came a Man who not only taught us a new way of life, but brought us into a new relationship with our Creator. [143

...**Meaning.** What is the real meaning of Christmas? A holiday which has survived 20 centuries of strife, struggle and sorrow certainly deserves our most serious thought. So great was the impact of Christ's advent that even non-Christian nations date their calendars according to it. Men discovered what it meant to have hope. Old prejudices were laid aside, superstitions were dispelled, and many of earth's people began to walk in "newness of life." Christmas means that God made contact with man, and revealed the length and depth of His forgiving love for a fallen race of men. [144

CHURCH

...**Attendance.** God is not impressed nor pleased by our weekly pilgrimages to His sanctuaries when we are unacquainted with judgment, mercy and faith. [145

A fire broke out in a small-town church. When the fire brigade, siren wailing, arrived on the spot the minister recognized one of the men. "Hello there, Jim—I haven't seen you in church for a long time," he chided. "Well," answered the sweating fireman, struggling with the hose, "there hasn't been a fire in church for a long time, preacher." [146

It is clear that the rate of crime is lower among people who actually go to church regularly. It is our Christian faith which alone gives ultimate meaning for morality. [147

... Attitude Toward. Many persons today insist on coming into the church head first rather than heart first.[148

... Church-Goers. Church-goers are like coals in a fire. When they cling together they keep the flame aglow; when they separate, they die out. [149

... Comfort. I am afraid that we in the church are making a great mistake by trying to make Christianity popular and pleasant. We have taken the cross away and substituted cushions. [150

... Concern. I am afraid the church is trying to speak out on too many issues that really do not concern the church. [151

... Definition. The church is Christ's organization upon earth. [152

... Denominations. In just about every Christian denomination, Christ is central. Regardless of the church we

44

attend, each of us should have a personal relationship with Jesus Christ. Christianity is not temples, creeds, and rituals —it is a Person, the Person of Jesus Christ. We may join every church in town, but if Christ is not real, we have missed the whole point of being a Christian. [153

... **Difficulties.** The difficulty in most churches is that we're spending so much of our time with secular issues, and on committees of various sorts dealing with secular issues, that we don't have time to deal with the spiritual problems that people face. [154

... **Failure.** I wonder if the church has not failed this generation of young people by failing to make the Christian faith the thrilling, joyful triumphant experience that it really is. [155

The church today has been so anxious to be intellectually respectable and have perfect decorum and security that the reality, joy and thrill of Christian experience have been overlooked and sometimes forgotten. [156

... **Membership.** The most difficult thing in the world is to get a man to see that he really needs Jesus Christ when he has lived for years with his name on a church roll but never really had a personal encounter with the living Christ. [157

... **Mission Of.** The changing of men is the primary mission of the church. The only way to change men is to get them converted to Jesus Christ. [158

45

...**Moral Problems.** The church speaks out on many social problems, but it has been strangely silent on the moral problems that face the nation. [159

...**Need.** What the church needs is not more machinery or better organizations or novel methods, but men whom God can use. [160

...**Need Of Revival.** The greatest need in the church today is a spiritual revival that will drive her back to her knees and will cause her earnestly to contend for the faith once delivered. [161

...**Negative Approach.** Often the church has banged away negatively at evils, but has left men vacuous, without reminding them that God is tremendously interested in our finding a satisfying, positive way of life. [162

...**Popularity.** When the Christian or the church becomes popular with the unbelieving world, something is seriously wrong with the Christian or the church.[163

...**Repentance.** I call upon the church today to fall on its knees before God, and ask the God of our salvation to lead on in a spiritual revolution that will shake America and the world. [164

...**Society; Politics.** There is a viewpoint prevailing in some areas of the church that its function is to change social structures, through political power and political pressure. In my opinion, this is not supported from the Bible. I think the

46

Biblical approach is to change men and men themselves will change society for the better. [165

... **Task Of.** I am convinced that if the church went back to its main task of preaching the Gospel and getting people converted to Christ it would have far more impact on the social structure of the nation than it can have in any other thing it could possibly do. [166

CIVIL RIGHTS

The evening that the Civil Rights Bill was passed, I had the honor of being present at the White House. Senator (now Vice President) Hubert Humphrey came into the room and walked to where I was standing. "Billy," he said, "we have the law on the books. Now it is the task of people like you to see that it works from the heart." [167

... **Attitude.** (Quoted from a speech at Clinton, Tenn., 1958): Hot heads and cold hearts never solved anything. [168

... **Church; Segregation.** It is impossible for me to understand how a church can hold segregated meetings. There are some churches that even Jesus Christ Himself might not be allowed into if He came back. For you see, Christ did not have a white skin, nor did He have as black a skin, perhaps, as the West African. He more than likely had tan skin, like the people of the Middle East. [169

... **Demonstrations.** I have been holding demonstrations for fifteen years, but in a stadium where it is legal.[170

... **Extremists.** If the Ku Klux Klan will quiet down, if the extremists in the civil rights organizations will give time to digest the new civil rights laws, and if the politicians will not try to exploit the situation, we will have a settlement of racial troubles. [171

COMMANDMENTS

... **Broken.** All of us have broken all the Commandments. Now, you might say, "I've never committed murder," for instance. But if there is hatred in your heart for your brother without cause, you have already committed murder. [172

... **Knowledge Of.** I think the new generation coming along is far better acquainted with Jayne Mansfield's statistics than it is with the Second Commandment which orders that "Thou shalt not make unto thee any image."[173

... **Sexual Freedom.** The commandments of God are obeyed by an ever decreasing number, while the ethic of sexual freedom is eagerly learned and still more eagerly practiced by ever increasing millions of men and women within the church itself. [174

COMMITMENT

It is disturbing that for millions of church members there is no deep commitment to the cause of Christ. [175

... **To Truth.** If some can be counted on to commit themselves to error and to evil, how much more should we who know Christ commit ourselves to the Truth. [176

48

COMMUNICATION

...God And Man. The communication between God and man seems to be broken. There exist joy, light, harmony, peace and satisfaction, yet millions of persons are blind and deaf, and even dead to them. People long for serenity and search for happiness, but never seem to find them, so they give up and surrender to pessimism.[177

...God To Man. Our television set may be sitting in the living room, cold, dark, and lifeless, but that is not the fault of the television industry. We must turn the dials of our set; we must tune in on the right channels. God is sending forth His messages of love, but we must tune in. We must be willing to listen and to receive His message and obey it. [178

COMMUNISM

...Defense. The best defense against communism is a citadel of strength through godliness and righteousness.[179

...Moral Effects. Satan's masterpiece in our times is the philosophy of communism. Its godless, materialistic interpretation of life has had untold effects upon the moral life of the nation. So damaging has been that philosophy on life that the eminent psychologist-physician, Dr. Oswald Schwarts, says, "Nothing short of a spiritual revolution would be sufficient to rectify the sexual as well as the other effects of our way of living. A purely economic revolution would not do, as the experience of Russia proved in the early years of the Soviets." [180

49

... **Scandinavia.** There is new respect for America in Scandinavia, because there is a feeling that we are going to stand firm against communism. [181

... **Weapons Against.** The greatest and most effective weapon against communism today is a true Christian. [182

COMPASSION

God wants Christians to be concerned and burdened for a lost world. [183

... **Basis Of.** God doesn't compare us to each other. He compares us to Jesus Christ, and all of us fall short of Jesus. [184

... **Gospel.** I have found that people everywhere, all over the world, will respond to the Gospel of Jesus Christ if we present it simply, with Christian compassion. [185

... **World's Needs.** Your eyes should become the eyes of the resurrected Christ, to exhibit His sympathy and tenderness. He wants to look on the world's needs through your eyes. [186

COMPROMISE

... **Christians.** The reason communism is making inroads in the world today is that somewhere along the line the people who were supposed to live Christian lives compromised their beliefs. [187

... **Tolerance.** Tolerance, in one sense, implies the compromise of one's convictions, a yielding of ground upon important issues. Over-tolerance in moral issues can make us soft, flabby and devoid of conviction. [188

CONCERN

When your ears become the ears of the resurrected Christ, they will be sensitive to every cry of spiritual need. [189

CONFESSION

Psychiatrists realize that there are curative powers in confession. [190

CONFLICT

... **Commitment.** There is a war going on within the human heart. God contends for a total commitment, for a surrender to His will. But in willfulness, because of our sinful nature, we contend for the free expression of our own will. Only when a soul abdicates to the will of God, will this war end. [191

CONFORMITY

Each of us has a tendency to gravitate toward a certain group and we have a tendency to conform and be like everybody else. Because everybody else is doing it we think that we ought to do it. [192

... **Compromise.** Satan's most effective tool is conformity and compromise. He is aware that one man standing in the midst of a pagan people, declaring, "I am not ashamed of the gospel of Christ: for it is the power of God unto salva-

51

tion," can move more people in the direction of God than thousands of insipid professors of religion.   [193

... **Human Nature.** Times have changed but human nature hasn't. Though the methods are different, the pagan world is still trying to put their stamp of conformity on every follower of Jesus Christ.   [194

... **Youth.** On campus today, conformity is the big thing. Nobody wants to be different. Everybody dresses like the other people. They sing the same song. Act the same way. Nobody wants to be different. But Jesus calls on you to be different. He calls on you to be honest, and pure and clean and wholesome. Not a prude. Somebody that can have a good time, yes—but different.   [195

CONSCIENCE

Conscience is our gentlest counselor and teacher and our most faithful friend.   [196

God has revealed Himself in man's conscience. Conscience has been described as the light of the soul.   [197

CONVERSATION

It is unfortunate that even among Christians, conversation is of comparatively small matters. We can quote the batting averages of our favorite baseball stars, but we are unable to quote a Bible verse other than John 3:16.   [198

CONVERSION

...**Completeness.** If you have an intellectual accept-ance of Christ, and an emotional experience—that still is not enough. There must be the conversion of the will   [199

...**Definition.** Conversion is that voluntary change in the mind of a sinner in which he turns on the one hand from sin and on the other hand to Christ.   [200

...**Effects Of.** True conversion will involve the total mind, the total affection and the total will.   [201

The converted person will love what he once hated, and hate what he once loved.   [202

...**Free Will.** No one can be converted except with the consent of his own free will, because God does not override human choice.   [203

...**Way To.** You get converted by admitting "I am a sinner," by acknowledging that you have broken God's laws and that you can't change your ways without God's help.   [204

COURAGE

All through history God has called upon men to be coura-geous in deed and word.   [205

...**Free Men.** Free men should never be content to be mute, cowardly, cramped and conformed.   [206

...**Moral.** It is my prayer today that we will recover our moral courage in this country. If we recover our moral courage, it will take a moral and a spiritual awakening that must sweep this country from coast to coast, like a prairie fire.   [207

. . . Need For. We need to stand up and be counted, or evil will take over this country.   [208

. . . War. Our world stands on the threshold of a nuclear war that could destroy much of civilization. If ever there was a time we needed men and women of courage to mobilize for Jesus Christ it is now.   [209

CRIMINALS

. . . Cause Of. The criminal is the product of a society which, though not altogether criminal, has lived sinfully and selfishly and has created an atmosphere conducive to the more rash criminal deeds.   [210

CRITICISM

A sin prevalent among Christians is the sin of criticism—going around and trying to take a speck out of our brother's eye when we have a log in our own.   [211

I make it a policy never to answer critics, but to go on in the way I know is God's will, preaching the everlasting Gospel of Christ.   [212

CROSS

Those who stand by the cross are those who change the course of history.   [213

... **Choice.** The cross Jesus talked about was one that a man must choose voluntarily and deliberately.   [214

... **Meaning.** To take up the cross means that you take your stand for the Lord Jesus no matter what it costs. [215

... **Neglect Of.** To neglect the cross of Christ, to ignore the eternity toward which we are all moving—this is the height of madness.   [216

... **Redemption.** The Cross of Christ is still an offense to unregenerate man, but it remains his only hope of redemption.   [217

CULTURE

Culture is a mollifying ointment rubbed on externally. It cannot reach down to man's deepest need anymore than vaseline can heal cancer.   [218

... **Danger.** Culture contains a subtle danger. It stresses the importance of appearances and superficialities and tends to neglect the soul's need of inner cleansing and forgiveness.   [219

CURIOSITY

Looking over the more than 2,000 persons who had come to hear me at a university student-faculty meeting, I noted that many had come out of curiosity. At such a meeting I can always count on the Department of Psychology showing up in full force.   [220

·· D ··

DANCING

Drinking fathers and frug-dancing mothers are responsible for the nation's rebellious teen-agers.　　[221

DARKNESS

Where a person has deviated from the eternal rules of God and morality, there is darkness. And while in darkness, he begins to pass false judgments upon most things of vital import. You, too, can reach such a state in your sinfulness that you can no longer tell the difference between good and evil.　　[222

DEATH

... **Christian.**　Death is the Christian's coronation, the end of conflict and the beginning of glory in heaven and triumph.　　[223

Though the Christian has no immunity from death and no claim to perpetual life on this planet, death is to him a friend rather than a foe—the beginning rather than the end —another step on the pathway to heaven rather than a leap into a dark unknown.　　[224

When a Christian dies, he goes straight into the presence of Christ. He goes to heaven to spend eternity with God. When a sinner dies, he goes into outer darkness, into a place that Jesus has called hell.   [225

...Dread Of. No matter how miserable a man's existence, he does not want to die. Death carries with it a certain dread. From the day that the first couple laid their first-born son in the grave, men have dreaded death.   [226

...Fear Of. The fear of death is a condition that is perfectly normal for any who have never come to Christ. Death is an experience from which we shrink, yet for the Christian, the fear is removed.   [227

...Inevitability; Reality. Men have tried to change the appearance of death by changing the word "undertaker" to "mortician"; "caskets" instead of "coffins"; "funeral homes" instead of "undertaking parlors"; and "memorial parks" instead of "cemeteries." We soften the starkness of the final rites. But no matter what we call it, or how we rouge the cheeks, the cold, hard, cruel reality and inevitability of death have not changed and will not change.   [228

...Kinds. The Bible indicates that there are three kinds of death: physical, spiritual and eternal.   [229

...Life After. In man's instinct something down inside says—there must be a future life—there must be something beyond this life. There is only one person who can speak

57

on this subject because He came from the grave; He rose and His name was Jesus Christ. [230

... Non-Christian. I have talked to doctors and nurses who have held the hands of dying people and they say that there is as much difference between the death of a Christian and a non-Christian as there is between heaven and hell. [231

... Reality Of. We try to cushion death's blow by taking out insurance and by other devices to make our last days comfortable; but the stark, dread reality of death is always staring us in the face. [232

DECEPTION

... Judas. Everybody thought Judas was on the road to heaven. But it turned out that when the chips were down, Judas denied his Lord, betrayed his Lord, and the Bible says he went to his own place, that he was never saved. Yet he was the treasurer of Jesus' church. Jesus only had twelve members. [233

... Satan. The underlying principle of all Satan's tactics is deception. He is a crafty and clever camouflager . . . He does not build a church and call it the First Church of Satan —he is far too clever for that. He invades the theological seminary and even the pulpit. Many times he even invades the church under the cover of an orthodox vocabulary, emptying sacred terms of their Biblical sense. [234

DECISION

Jesus says there is a narrow road that leads to eternal life and a broad road that leads to destruction. There are people on both roads. A choice must be made. You can't go both. [235

DEFEAT

... **Christian.** From the divine viewpoint, the defeated Christian is a monstrosity. He is abnormal. [236

DEMONSTRATIONS

... **Anti U. S. Demonstrations In South America.** This is the beginning of a world-wide wave against us, the handi-work of a small, well-organized minority. We need to repent. Our sins are many. [237

DEPRAVITY

Man is born with a sinful nature, and unless it is trans-formed by the power of God, it is capable of indescribable brutality and evil. [238

The totality of depravity existing in men is having its normal fruitage in a social order so complicated, confused, and corrupted that only the return of Christ can save it.[239

DEVIL

Do you believe in the devil? Jesus talked about it. The whole Bible talks about it. I believe he exists and I believe he tempts me every day of my life. He troubles me at every turn. [240

... **Lies.** The devil starts many deliberate lies about God's servants and thousands of Christians grasp them, be-lieve them, and pass them along in ugly gossip. [241

... Objective. The Bible teaches that the devil is a real person and that he controls the affairs of this evil world. His great objective is to defeat the will and program of God in the world, in the church and in the Christian.   [242

DISCIPLES

The men who followed Christ were unique in their generation. They turned the world upside down because their hearts had been turned right side up.   [243

DISCIPLESHIP

... Cost. Salvation is free, but discipleship costs everything we have.   [244

DISCIPLINE

... Children. The word discipline means "to teach." The job of teaching has been too long left to the school teacher and the scoutmaster. Parents, your job is to teach your children, by precept and example, to be good members of the household, good citizens of the community, good members of the church and followers of Jesus Christ.   [245

... Home. Be certain that there is loving Christian discipline in the home. The most effective way for parents to command obedience is by a clean, pure, wholesome, Christian example.   [246

... Parental. Proper discipline in the home is the product of love and concern. How can we say that we love our children when we see them become more disrespectful of authority, more irreverent and more barbaric and do nothing about it? Many psychiatrists today are beginning to realize that children do need discipline. [247

... **Personal.** The effective Christians of history have been men and women of great personal discipline—mental discipline, discipline of the body, discipline of the tongue, and discipline of the emotion. [248

... **Reason.** God does not discipline us to subdue us, but to condition us for a life of usefulness and blessedness. [249

... **Sin Of Tolerance.** A compass is narrow-minded—it always points to the magnetic north. It seems that is a very narrow view, but a compass is not broad-minded. If it were, all the ships at sea and all the planes in the air would be in danger. We must discipline ourselves, personally, to fight any deviation from the course Jesus set for us. We cannot be tolerant of any other course. To deviate is to sin. [250

DISCOURAGEMENT

... **Cure For.** You will never be free from discouragement and despondency until you have been tuned to God. Christ is the Well-Spring of happiness. He is the Fountain-Head of joy. [251

... **Despondency.** Christ can take discouragement and despondency out of your life. He can put a spring in your step and give you a thrill in your heart and a purpose in your mind. Optimism and cheerfulness are products of knowing Christ. [252

61

DISHONESTY

Dishonesty's disease invades every profession and its spread into our society is alarming, even to the most apathetic among us. [253

DISOBEDIENCE

At the very root of every problem that besets us is the absence of the knowledge of God and man's refusal to obey Him. [254

DISUNITY

... **Christian.** The greatest excuse given to me by people in every country for not becoming Christians is the division among Christians today. [255

... **Confusion.** Unbelievers are confused as they gaze upon the strife within and between religious bodies. [256

DIVORCE

Reno can give you a quick divorce, but Christ can give you a quick transformation in your home. The tempers that have flared, the irritations that are evident, the unfaithfulness that is suspected, the monotony and boredom of existence without love can be changed and transformed in the twinkling of an eye by faith in Jesus Christ. [257

... **Politics.** There was a time when a divorced man would have no chance in American politics, but with our shifting ideals of today, whether or not a person is divorced seems to make little difference. [258

. . . Record. France has only one-fourth the number of divorces we do; Germany has only one-third, and Japan has only one-half the number of broken homes that we Americans have. [259

. . . Statistics. Where did these divorces and broken homes come from? A recent survey found only one divorce to every 57 marriages took place where the families were regular church attendants. The national divorce rate is one out of three. It was also found that only one divorce in 500 marriages took place where there was regular daily Bible reading and prayer in the home. This amazing survey gives us two significant facts: that divorces in America are mostly among non-religious people, and a Christian home is the best possible insurance against a broken home. [260

DOGS

. . . Husbands. Dogs are quick to show their affection. They never pout, they never bear a grudge. They never run away from home when mistreated. They never complain about their food. They never gripe about the way the house is kept. They are chivalrous and courageous, ready to protect their mistress at the risk of their lives. They love children, and no matter how noisy and boisterous they are, the dog loves every minute of it. In fact, a dog is stiff competition for a husband. Perhaps if we husbands imitated a few of our dog's virtues, life with our family might be more amiable. [261

DOUBT

Doubt is the disease of this inquisitive, restless age. It is the price we pay for our advanced intelligence and civilization—the dim night of our resplendent day. But as the most beautiful light is born of darkness, so the faith that springs from conflict is often the strongest and the best. [262

· · E · ·

EASTER

Even though Easter has been commercialized, to the genuine Christian it is still the hope of his immortality. [263

...**Christianity.** Easter makes Christianity distinctive and unique and sets it apart from all world religions. [264

...**Mary Magdalene.** Mary Magdalene is one of the miracles of Easter, that God could take a besmirched woman and forgive her. [265

...**Resurrection.** The further we get from the fact of the Resurrection, the closer we get to the reality of destruction. [266

EASY WAY

We are looking constantly for the easy way out. There is a striking parallel between present-day conditions in America and that of Rome in her last years. [267

ECUMENICAL MOVEMENT

The Council provided for a new reformation—or freedom —within the Church of Rome. [268

The Ecumenical Council meetings in Rome have healed many of the wounds of 400 years and eased tensions between Protestants and Catholics throughout the world.[269

ECUMENICITY

I have often wondered if all the different denominations are pleasing to God. When Jesus left this world, didn't He command that His apostles carry on His work? In Chapter 17 of John He prayed that the disciples might be one. Has this prayer of Jesus been in vain?   [270

ECUMENISM

... **Evangelism.** I believe it is possible in mass evangelism to reach a "depth of ecumenism" that is more significant in some ways even than organization ecumenism.   [271

EDUCATION

... **Failure.** Our educational system has failed. We are so intent on imparting knowledge, but so lax in instilling the power to direct that knowledge toward constructive goals, we have built bone without sinew; generated energy without purpose; imparted knowledge without wisdom; developed minds and bodies, but neglected the soul. Thus, young people have no rock upon which to build their lives. Thousands are restless, floundering and confused.   [272

... **Higher.** Higher education has never enjoyed a level of efficiency and performance so high and a level of influence so low.   [273

. . . Limitations. To educate a man without moral and spiritual strength, is to educate a savage. This is one of the most dangerous aspects of communism, and we are in danger of copying the Communists by educating the minds and building the body with physical fitness programs, but neglecting the spiritual and moral side of man. This is why I so violently disagree with those who would throw God and religion out of our schools.   [274

. . . Problems. We've taken God out of the schools and put sex in. And I think that this is causing many of our problems among young people.   [275

. . . Religion; Harvard. Our educational institutions were founded on a religious concept and faith in God. Look at Harvard University: In his bequest, Mr. Harvard left several rules and precepts that were to be observed by the college. The second rule reads as follows: "Let every student be plainly instructed and earnestly pressed to consider well the main ends of his life and studies. To know God in Jesus Christ, which is eternal life, and therefore to lay Christ in the bottom of the only foundation of all knowledge and learning; and, seeing the Lord only giveth wisdom, let everyone seriously set himself by prayer in secret to seek it of Him."   [276

. . . Young People. The young person who takes a dim view of education is really curtailing his future earning power, and while I have heard of people saying they could live on love, I know of no documented record of anyone ever having done it.   [277

ENTHUSIASM

...Need Of. One of the great needs in the church today is for every Christian to become enthusiastic about his faith in Jesus Christ. [278

...Spiritual. It is very strange that the world accepts enthusiasm in every realm but the spiritual. [279

ENVY

Envy takes the joy, happiness and contentment out of living. [280

...Consequence Of. There is a Greek story about a man who killed himself through envy. His fellow citizens had erected a statue to one of their number who was a celebrated champion in the public games. But this man, a rival of the honored athlete, was so envious that he vowed that he would destroy that statue. Every night he went out into the darkness and chiseled at its base in an effort to undermine its foundation and make it fall. At last he succeeded. It did fall —but it fell on him. He fell, a victim of his own envy. [281

...Disease Of. If you were to find the germs of tuberculosis lurking in your body, you would spare no time, effort or money in ruling them out. And yet, many people are afflicted with this deadly, venomous envy, and they are doing nothing about it! [282

...Inherent. Envy, according to the Bible, is inherent in our very nature. We read in James 4:5, "The spirit that dwelleth in us, lusteth to envy." Cain envied Abel because he had found favor with God—and then murdered him. Envy needs no justification to make an attack. More often than not, there is no real reason for its existence. It springs from the unregenerate human heart as naturally as weeds grow in a flower garden. [283

... **Jealousy.** Envy and jealousy can ruin reputations, split churches and cause murders. Envy can shrink our circle of friends, ruin our business and dwarf our souls. [284

ESCAPE

... **Despondency.** Despondency leads many persons on a frantic round of cocktail parties and, sometimes, on to narcotics. It is the pattern of man's desperate search to find an escape from the cold realities of sin-blighted existence. Yet, all the while, God is there, speaking and beckoning. [285

ESCHATOLOGY

For the past few years, church leaders have been afraid of fanaticism in the discussion of future events, but the church is taking a new look at these reams of Holy Scripture that talk about the future-events' course of human history. [286

ETERNITY

The more we doubt the Bible, the less awareness we have of eternity; and the more we believe it, the more conscious we are of the vast unknown to which no sane man would venture without God. [287

... **Preparation For.** What a wonderful thing to know

that if in my sleep tonight I should be taken out into eternity, or in an automobile wreck, I'm ready to meet God. Are you? [288

ETHICS

If we embrace a spiritual, aesthetic gospel only, and disregard our obligation to our fellow men, we annul it all. With an acceptance of Christ must go a practice of Christian ethics. [289

EVANGELISM

... Churches. If all churches were engaged in perennial evangelism, I don't think there would ever be need for a person like me. [290

... Giving. The entire world could be evangelized overnight if Christian people would give as the Lord has prospered them. [291

... World-Wide Need. We need Christ in every phase of our lives. Christ must be taken out into the marketplace, into our halls of learning, into our legislative assemblies. Christ must be taken to Africa, where a continent is being engulfed in an inferno of changes. Christ must be taken to Asia, where people are starving not only for food but for a fuller and richer way of life. [292

... World-Wide Revival. One of the greatest and most far-reaching social revolutions of history was directly related to, and grew out of, the great evangelical revivals of the 18th century. I believe that a great spiritual revival today would have social consequences around the world. [293

EVIDENCE OF GOD

Whenever anyone asks me how I can be so certain about who and what God really is, I am reminded of the story of the little boy who was out flying a kite. It was a fine day for kite flying, the wind was brisk and large billowy clouds were blowing across the sky. The kite went up and up until it was entirely hidden by the clouds.

"What are you doing?" a man asked the little boy.

"I'm flying a kite," he replied.

"Flying a kite, are you?" the man said. "How can you be sure? You can't see your kite."

"No," said the boy, "I can't see it, but every little while I feel a tug, so I know for sure that it's there!"

Don't take anyone else's word for God. Find Him for yourself, and then you too will know by the wonderful, warm tug on your heartstrings that He is there for sure.   [294

EXPERIENCE

. . . Value Of.   Parents can explain the law of gravity and the danger of climbing, but the child learns more about the law of gravity when he falls out of a tree than he does from the lips of his elders.   [295

EXTREMISM

We cannot survey the history of the human race without marveling at the persistence of men and women whom the world called mad.   [296

Men and women of enthusiasm disturb the complacent, the smug, and the apathetic; and so the people, with their heads buried in the sand, pass judgment, calling them mad, beside themselves.   [297

. . . Sanity. The really sane people are often those at whom the world laughs and despises. As we look back on Christ we can see that it was He who was sane, and His critics who were mad. [298

.. F ..

FAITH

After we have examined all the evidence, we still must take that final step on simple childlike faith.   [299

...**Assurance.**   Paul and Silas had something inside of them that caused them to sing in the midst of the troubles and trials and difficulties of life. How wonderful it is to be able to face the temptations and struggles of life with joy and anticipation, with assurance, with security!   [300

...**Demonstration Of.**   You best demonstrate your faith in a bank by putting your money in it. You best show your faith in a doctor by trusting him in times of illness. You best prove your faith in a boat by getting aboard. You best demonstrate your faith in Christ by trusting Him with your life and receiving Him unconditionally as your Savior. [301

...**God.**   Faith is the only approach man has to God.   [302

...**Intellect.**   Faith is not anti-intellectual. It is an act of man that reaches beyond the limits of our five senses. [303

... Life. The Christian life is dependent upon faith. We stand on faith; we live by faith. Without faith, there is nothing. [304

... Mental Illness. Today one-half of all the hospital beds in America are occupied by mental patients. And half of those mental patients are there because they lack faith. They don't have a purpose for existence—a reason for living. Only faith can give them that "reason to be." [305

... Obstacle. The church gets bogged down and itself becomes a real stumbling block to faith. [306

... Salvation. Faith is the avenue to salvation. Not intellectual understanding. Not money. Not your works. Just simple faith. How much faith? The faith of a mustard seed, so small you can hardly see it. But if you will put that little faith in the person of Jesus, your life will be changed. He will come with supernatural power into your heart. It can happen to you. [307

FAMILY

... Duties. The Bible outlines very carefully the duties of husband, wife and children. The Bible warns that if you depart from these regulations concerning the governmental arrangement of the family, you will be in serious difficulty and the happiness of your home will be in danger. [308

... Home. The family should be a closely knit group. The home should be a self-contained shelter of security; a kind of school where life's basic lessons are taught; a kind of church where God is honored; a place where wholesome recreation and simple pleasures are enjoyed.   [309

...**Worship.** Establish a daily family worship. Say a prayer of thanksgiving at each meal. Have a special time in the morning or evening when all the family gathers together to hear the Bible read and have prayer.   [310

FATALISM

I knew two brothers who lived in the mountains. One of them always said: "I believe what is to be will be." The other said: "God helps those who help themselves." The first is still lodged in his mountain cabin, whittling away his life. The other is a surgeon, ministering to the needs of suffering humanity, and is an accepted, honored member of his community.   [311

FATHER

...**Biblical Definition.** According to the Bible, the male parent was created for much more than just to help bring in financial support. He was created as the human counterpart of God Himself.   [312

FATHERS

...**Children.** Take time with your children, for the sins of a father visit in the next generation. But if your child goes astray and you have reared him according to the word of God, the Bible says when he's old he'll come back.   [313

... Example. Many fathers are good at lecturing and preaching to their children, but they are not good at setting an example daily in front of them. [314

... Family Morality. If society is to be saved from the moral morass into which it is slowly sinking, fathers are going to have to take their God-given place at home. One of the greatest needs in America is for men who will muster the moral courage and appropriate the spiritual strength to lead their families by example and precept in the ways of God and character building. [315

... Responsibility In Home. God holds fathers responsible for the spiritual life in your home. I want to ask you this: Do you have daily prayer in your home? Is there Bible reading in your home? Is grace said at the table at every meal? If not, God will hold the man responsible. [316

FELLOWSHIP

... Dinners. I think the church fellowship dinners are a fine thing. Jesus ate with His disciples in the Upper Room, and I believe there is something edifying about God's people eating and fellowshipping together. [317

FORGIVENESS

Christ will forgive all the past. That is why He died on the cross. When those nails went into His hands, it was for you. He took the judgment, the hell, the death, the suffering that you and I deserve because of sin. [318

Only as we bow in contrition, confession and repentance at the foot of the Cross, can we find forgiveness.   [319

...**Christians.**   Forgiveness is as natural for the Christian as it is contrary for the non-Christian.   [320

FREEDOM
...**Love Of.**   Those who have a true love of freedom will do everything in their power to keep the freedom that they have.   [321

...**Of Speech.**   We have in our hands the most potent weapon God has ever given man—freedom of speech. But with this great freedom must go a strong sense of responsibility for what we say.   [322

...**Speaking Out.**   Freedom of speech means nothing to a people who are too weak in their convictions to speak out against the evil that is eating at the heart of the nation like a cancer.   [323

FREE WILL
...**Choice.**   When God granted man the power of choice, He took the risk of man choosing evil instead of good; death instead of life, and self-destruction instead of salvation.   [324

FRIENDS

... **Christ.** You cannot say that you are friendless when Christ has said, "Henceforth I call you not servants . . . but I have called you friends" (John 15:15).   [325

FUTURE

... **Life.** The Christian believes in a fabulous future, even though the present structure of modern society should disappear and all its progress should be wiped out by self-destruction as a result of man's failure. There is a sense in which the Kingdom of God is already here in the living presence of Christ in the hearts of all true believers. There is also, however, the ultimate consummation of all things, which is called the Kingdom of God. This is the fabulous future!   [326

··G··

GAMBLING

Most professional gamblers began their careers as petty gamblers, just as most alcoholics began drinking moderately. The appeal of gambling is somewhat understandable. There is something alluring about getting something for nothing. I realize that. And that is where the sin lies. Gambling of any kind amounts to "theft" by permission. The coin is flipped, the dice are rolled, or the horses run, and somebody rakes in that which belongs to another. The Bible says: "In the sweat of thy face shalt thou eat bread." It doesn't say, "By the flip of a coin, shalt thou eat thy lunch." I realize that in most petty gambling, no harm is intended. But the principle is the same as in big gambling. The difference is only in the amount of money involved. [327

GENTLENESS

The word gentle was rarely heard before the Christian era, and the word gentleman was not known. This high quality of character was a direct by-product of Christian faith. [328

GERMANY

... **Nazism.** Nazism blossomed in Germany only after

79

the church had failed to fill the vacuum which followed World War I. When the church failed to present and declare a dynamic, living Christ, Germany was robbed of a Savior and gave birth to a dictator. [329

GIFTS

... **Giving.** God has given us two hands—one to receive with and the other to give with. We are not cisterns made for hoarding; we are channels made for sharing. If we fail to fulfill this divine duty and privilege, we have missed the meaning of Christmas. [330

GIVING

... **A Way of Preaching.** We can preach by giving to others so they may preach. Missionary gifts, church offerings, and charitable contributions all speak eloquently of your unselfishness and Christian generosity. [331

... **Christians.** If every Christian were giving "as he purposeth in his heart, not grudgingly, or of necessity,"—but cheerfully as God has prospered him—there would be more than enough to advance the kingdom of God in this most critical period of human history. [332

... **Selfishness.** The key word of the selfish, unregenerate person is *get*. The key word of the dedicated Christian should be *give*. [333

... **Spiritual.** The greatest blessing of giving is not on the financial side of the ledger, but on the spiritual side. It gives a sense of being honest with God. [334

GLUTTONY

Gluttony is the epitome of human selfishness . . . a perversion of a natural God-given appetite. It is a sin because it is a physical expression of the philosophy of materialism. It is a sin that most of us commit, but few of us ever mention. [335

GOD

... **Aid To Man.** God has not promised to deliver us from trouble; but He has promised to stand by us through any troubles we might ever face. [336

... **As A Person.** The Bible not only reveals God as Spirit, undiscerned by human hearts and untouched by human hands, but the Bible also reveals God as a Person. Everywhere in the Bible we read: "God loves"; "God says"; "God does." Everything that we attribute to a person is attributed to God. [337

... **Characteristics.** The Bible tells us that God is Omnipotent. That means that He has all power. The Bible tells us that He is Omnipresent. That means that He is everywhere at the same time. The Bible tells us that He is Omniscient. That means that He has all knowledge. He knows everything that you do. "His eye is on the sparrow," and if God the Spirit is watching the sparrow, how much more He is watching you every moment. [338

... **Concept Of.** I believe that man's concept of God began with our first parents, because we are told in the Bible that they were created by God. [339

...Crucifixion. God proved His love on the cross. When Christ hung, and bled, and died it was God saying to the world—I love you. [340

...Defined. Jesus defined God as a spirit. That doesn't mean that a spirit doesn't have personality, because the Bible teaches that God definitely has personality and all the attributes of personality. If God had a body like yours or mine, He'd be confined to one place at one time, or one planet at one time. But because He is a spirit, He fills all of space, and He can be everywhere at the same time. [341

...Denial Of. Once man denies the existence of God, he can stoop to anything. [342

...Description. The Bible teaches that there was no time when God did not exist. He has been as He is—forever. He has no beginning and no end. He is the Eternal and Unchanging Person. [343

...Fellowship With. You were made for God's fellowship, and to fulfill any other purpose is to fail to fulfill your destiny. [344

...Finding Him. It is impossible to find God through the intellectual processes alone. If we try, we end up being ridiculous and foolish. The Bible teaches that we "must believe that He is." [345

...Friendship. God's children are guaranteed the richest and truest friendship both here and hereafter. [346

...Hate. We in the church have failed to remind this generation that while God is love, He also has the capacity to hate. He hates sin. [347

...His Law. As the Constitution is the highest law of the land, so the Bible is the highest law of God. [348

...Hunger For. You were created in the image and likeness of God. You were made for God's fellowship, and your heart can never be satisfied without His communion. Just as iron is attracted to a magnet, the soul in its state of hunger is drawn to God. [349

...In Nature. There is a language in nature that speaks of the existence of God. It is the language of order, beauty, perfection and intelligence. [350

...Judgment. The law judges sin according to the act, but God judges us according to the evil in our hearts. [351

...Knowing. I believe I know God. And I believe that there are tens of millions of people throughout the world today that know God as their own. They are certain because He lives in their hearts. [352

...Laws. God's laws have never been amended. They cannot be adulterated by man or by man's attempts at "interpretation"—for God's laws are absolute. [353

...Man's Feelings. Why is it that we are encouraged to feel deeply about sports, politics, entertainment, literature, art, music—in fact, about anything except our faith in God? [354

...Moral Evil. The love of God will force us to take sides when confronted with moral evil. If we love the underprivileged, we will want to destroy the slums and ghettos that have no place in affluent America. If we love the young people of America, we will do everything in our power to destroy the things that hurt their character and jeopardize their future. [355

...Mystery Of. If you try to rationalize God exhaustively, you will fail. There are mysteries about God that we will never understand in this life. How can the small and finite, limited to time and space, understand an infinite God! [356

...Partnership. The Bible teaches that God has considered man a working partner. [357

...Partners With. If we are to be working partners with God, there are a few things which we should know, lest there be any misunderstanding. First, we should remember that God is the sole owner of the business. Second, we are stewards of our talents. Third, we are to be stewards of our money. [358

...Patience. God is a patient God. He is not willing that any should perish. [359

...Power. With God nothing is impossible. No task is

too arduous, no problem is too difficult, no burden is too heavy for His love. [360

... **Power Of.** God takes the weak and makes them strong. He takes the vile and makes them clean. He takes the worthless and makes them worthwhile. He takes the sinful and makes them sinless. [361

... **Separation From.** The Bible teaches us that every person born into the world is born in sin and is by nature a child of wrath. We are all separated from God and in ourselves utterly helpless, even though this natural man often puts up a religious front and endeavors by his own effort to please God. [362

... **Unlimited.** There is no limit to God. There is no limit to His wisdom. There is no limit to His power. There is no limit to His love. There is no limit to His mercy. [363

... **Voice Of.** Too long you have been listening to the voice of the diplomat, the scientist, the psychiatrist, the sociologist and the military commander. It is time you listened to the voice of Almighty God. [364

There are many ways by which God leads us but it is only when our minds and hearts have surrendered to Him that we sometimes hear His voice. [365

... **Wrath Of.** God used the wrath of men to work out His purpose with His people. There is no reason to believe that He will not let the axe of judgment fall on our heads if

we, like Israel, refuse to repent of our sins and turn to Jesus
Christ.   [366

"GOD IS DEAD" MOVEMENT

God is not only alive—God is laughing at the silly arguments of the supposedly learned men who lead this movement.   [367

... **Barth, Karl.** Dr. Karl Barth, the dean of European
theologians, in a scathing denunciation of modern theological writers says: "They have thrown out the baby with the
bath water. In trying to make Christianity possible for skep-
tics, they have succeeded only in making it meaningless." To
sum it all up, this is a false religion—it is another gospel.   [368

... **History.** This movement is not new, as many professors and students may suppose. On April 22, 1851, Auguste
Comte declared the death of God. Karl Marx said that
religion was the opiate of the people. He had a great deal in
common with the so-called radical theologians who are denying the existence of a personal God today. Even the expression "God is dead" is not new. It was first used by Nietzsche
in the nineteenth century.   [369

... **Jesus.** The "God is dead" cult wants to get rid of God
while retaining Jesus. This is a contradiction. It is anti-
scriptural; it is anti-Christian; and it is anti-intellectual. It is
impossible to hold on to the historical Jesus without God,
because Jesus without God is not Jesus.   [370

86

... Refuted. I sometimes feel a little like a West Coast cowboy and songwriter when someone told him that God was dead. He grabbed him by his coat and said, "Buddy, you're wrong; I just finished talking to Him."   [371

... Satan. Satan wants to get us to believe anything but the truth. But I think, personally, he's overstepped himself with these "God is dead" people, because they are arousing such religious interest in the country now that people are beginning to search their faith: "Why do I believe in God?" This is where, throughout history, Satan many times makes his big mistakes. He goes too far.   [372

... Theology; Confusion. A lot of people don't receive Christ because of theology. They read Dr. So-and-So who says God is dead. They read German writers who say everything is a myth. And they read this one and they read that one, and they get all confused. I say: forget all those men. Come to the Bible for the answer because you will never be able to prove the existence of God intellectually. You'll never be able to prove Christianity intellectually. You'll never be able to take God into a laboratory and put Him into a test tube.   [373

... What the Bible Says. Twice in the Psalms the Bible says, "The fool hath said in his heart, 'There is no God.' " In the second Psalm, it says, "He that sitteth in the heavens shall laugh." In other words, this spectacle, this ridiculous spectacle of man denying God—the Bible says God laughs.   [374

...Youth; Church. I am devoting time to this "God is dead" cult because many seminary students, university students and other people are being disturbed. They are wondering if the church is giving up its faith. Some young people are saying, "The church itself doesn't know what it believes any longer. Why should we concern ourselves with God, Christ or morality?" I want to assure you that these radical views do not represent the majority view of the church. They represent only a small, vocal group that is being given publicity because their views are so far-out and so radical. [375

GOLF

(To a top professional golfer) The game you play and the one I play ought to be called by two different names. [376

...Handicap. To me the whole game is a handicap. [377

...Religion. I have read many books on golf, but none of them improves my game. I must get out on the course and play. You may study theology and religion, but there comes a time when you must experience Christ for yourself. [378

GOOD FRIDAY

Earth never knew a darker day than that first Good Friday when the Prince of Glory died. But earth's most tragic day was transformed into earth's gladdest day for it marked the end of sin and checked its rule over the hearts and lives of earth's people. When Jesus lifted up His voice and shouted: "It is finished," He did not mean that His life was ebbing away or that God's plan had been foiled. Though death was near He realized that the last obstacle had been hurdled, the last enemy had been destroyed, and that He had successfully and triumphantly completed the task of redemption. [379

GOSPEL

The Gospel works anywhere and everywhere. It has been declared on every continent of the earth, under every possible social and economic condition, and it always produces the same fruit. [380

...**Composition.** The fact that the Lord Jesus died to save is one-half of the Gospel. The fact that He rose from the dead is the other half of the Gospel. [381

...**Human Destiny.** The good news of the Gospel solves the problem of human destiny, the most fundamental problem of human existence. [382

...**Intellectuals.** Many modern churchmen are accommodating themselves to the thought of our times, but Paul confronted the intellectuals of his day with the Gospel of Christ. We must proclaim the same message, and can count on the same divine consequences. [383

...**Religion.** At its best, religion can only succeed in producing an outward reformation. The Gospel commences by creating an inward transformation. [384

...**Religions.** There are thousands of religions, but there is only one Gospel. [385

...Unchanging. Among the basic things that have never changed are human nature, the Gospel, which is God's remedy for it, and the Holy Spirit, who is the agent of divine communication. [386

GOSSIP

If you gossip in front of your children, they are going to grow up to be gossipers. [387

...Sinfulness. Gossip, even about incidents that seem very minor, is a serious sin. [388

GRACE

Grace is not sought nor bought nor wrought. It is a free gift of Almighty God to needy mankind. [389

Real genuine, victorious living begins when the grace of God appears in its beauty and significance to you, when you actually commit and surrender your life to Jesus Christ.[390

...Motive. The motive of grace is the infinite, compassionate love of a merciful God, but the work of grace was the death of Christ on the Cross. [391

...Results. If you want something in your heart that will put a spring in your step and a smile on your face, then receive Jesus Christ as your personal Savior. Receive the gift of God's grace, and your life can be transformed from despondency to joy, victory and happiness. [392

...Source. We grow in grace and tap the source of spiritual strength by reading and studying the Word of God. We are actually changed by the Word which is the source of all Grace. [393

GREED

...Idolatry. The Bible teaches that greed is idolatry. [394

GUILT

...Conscience. To have a guilty conscience is a feeling. Psychologists may define it as a guilt complex, and may seek to rationalize away the sense of guilt, but once it has been awakened through the application of the law of God, no explanation will quiet the insistent voice of conscience.[395

...Sin. The conscience of man is often beyond the grasp of the psychiatrist. With all of his techniques, he cannot sound its depravity and depth. Man himself is helpless to detach himself from the gnawing guilt of a heart bowed down with the weight of sin. But where man has failed, God has succeeded. [396

· · H · ·

HAPPINESS

You may search the world over for contented and happy men, but you will find them only where Christ has been personally and decisively received. [397

... **Christianity.** Christianity was never meant to be something to make people miserable, but rather something to make them happy. [398

... **Source.** True happiness is from within, and does not depend on outward circumstances. When our sense of well-being depends on the things around us, we are in bad straits. [399

HEALTH

... **Exercise.** I run through the early morning of each day to develop the stamina I need. Our bodies are like trees —when the trunk goes, everything goes. St. Paul said much the same thing centuries ago: "Your body is a temple of the Holy Spirit." So glorify God in your body. [400

HEART

... **Man.** The heart of man is filthy and needs the

cleansing that only Christ can give. The heart of man is guilty and needs the forgiveness that only Christ can give. Without God, the best man in the world is capable of the most terrifying crimes. [401

... **Sin.** What does God see when He looks in your heart? Does He see lust, jealousy, hatred, anger, bitterness? Does He see a heart filled with sin? You probably think your heart is clean, but sin is universal. Every man is a sinner. [402

HEART OF MAN

Two conflicting forces cannot exist in one human heart. When doubt reigns, faith cannot abide. What hatred rules, love is crowded out. Where selfishness rules, there love cannot dwell. When worry is present, trust cannot crowd its way in. [403

HEAVEN

I'm not going to heaven because I've preached to great crowds of people. I'm going to heaven because Christ died on that cross. None of us are going to heaven because we're good. And we're not going to heaven because we've worked. We're not going to heaven because we pray and accept Christ. We're going to heaven because of what He did on the Cross. All I have to do is receive Him. And it's so easy to receive Christ that millions stumble over its sheer simplicity. [404

... **Description.** Heaven will be what we have always longed for. It will be the new social order that men dream of. All the things that have made earth unlovely and tragic will

93

be absent in heaven. There will be no night, no death, no disease, no sorrow, no tears, no ignorance, no disappointment, no war. It will be filled with happiness, worship, love, perfection and other good qualities. Heaven will be a place to challenge the creative genius of the unfettered mind of redeemed man.   [405

... **Entrance To.**   No man will ever be in heaven who did not by faith receive Christ as a personal Savior.   [406

... **Eternal Life.**   For the Christian, the grave is not the end; nor is death a calamity, for he has a glorious hope—the hope of Heaven.   [407

... **Family; Friends.**   If you are a Christian, you are going to see again those who have accepted Christ. In heaven, families and friends will be reunited.   [408

... **Home.**   The Bible takes the word "home," with all of its tender associations and with all of its sacred memories, and applies it to the hereafter and tells us that heaven is home.   [409

... **Money.**   Heaven in this life, and heaven in the life to come are not on a monetary standard.   [410

HEBREW

... **Old Testament Prophecy.**   The Hebrew faith prepared the way for the coming of Jesus Christ, and I believe that He was the fulfillment of scores and scores of passages in the Old Testament. He constantly quoted the Old Testament to show that He Himself was the fulfillment.   [411

HELL

   ... **Biblical Meaning.** There are four words that have been translated "hell" in our Bible. One word is "Sheol," which in the Old Testament is translated 31 times as "hell." It means an unseen state—a shadowy underworld. Words of sorrow, pain and destruction are used in connection with it. The second word is "Hades," which is translated from the Greek and is used ten times in the New Testament. It means the same as the Hebrew word "Sheol" in the Old Testament. Judgment and suffering are always connected with it. The third word is "Tartarus," used only once, in 2 Peter 2:4, where it says that disobedient angels are cast into "Tartarus." It indicates a place of judgment such as a prison or dungeon where there is intense darkness. The fourth word is "Gehenna," used 11 times in the New Testament and translated as "hell." It is the illustration that Jesus used of the Valley of Hinnom, a place outside Jerusalem where rubbish and debris burned continually.   [412

   ... **Choice.** God will never send anybody to hell. If man goes to hell, he goes by his own free choice. Hell was created for the devil and his angels, not for man. God never meant that man should go there. And God has done everything within His power to keep you out. He even gave His Son to die on that cross to keep you out. Because, you see, when God made you, He made you a free moral agent. You can live any kind of life you want to. You can live a good life, you can live a bad life. You can break all God's laws or you can obey them. You can go to heaven—or to hell. The choice is yours. [413

...**Church.** The doctrine of hell is not only unpopular in the church—it is almost forgotten. In glancing through the books in my library, I found that there have not been many sermons on this subject in the past 25 years. [414

...**Definition.** No matter how excruciating or how literal the fire of hell may or may not be, the thirst of a lost soul for the living water will be more painful than the fires of perdition. Hell, essentially and basically, is banishment from the presence of God for deliberately rejecting Jesus Christ as Lord and Savior. [415

...**Fact Of.** I find no pleasure in the knowledge of the fact of hell, but I find it my solemn duty to remind you that the same book that proclaims the wonders of heaven also describes the terrors of eternal banishment from God. [416

...**Use As A Word.** The word "hell" is used in thousands of conversations in hundreds of different ways every day. [417

HINDU
...**Christianity.** A Hindu leader once said to me, "When I see Christianity lived, I will become a Christian." [418

HISTORY
...**Lesson Of.** The lesson of history tells us that no

state or government devised by man can flourish forever.   [419

...**Value.** History is recorded so that we may avoid the
errors of the past.   [420

HOLY SPIRIT

...**Definition.** The Bible teaches that the Holy Spirit is
co-equal with God the Father and co-equal with God the
Son. The Bible also teaches that the Holy Spirit is a Person.
He is never to be referred to as "it." He's not just an agent.
He's not just an influence. He is a mighty Person: the Holy
Spirit of God.   [421

...**His Work.** The Bible tells us something of the work
of the Holy Spirit. What does He do? We are told in John
16:8 that He convicts men of sin: "And when He is come,
He will reprove the world of sin, and of righteousness, and
of judgment." That's the reason that before you can come to
Christ, you must acknowledge that you are a sinner. You
must renounce your sins. It is the Holy Spirit that convicts
you of your sin. He makes you feel uncomfortable. He pricks
your conscience. He makes you acknowledge and admit to
yourself that you are a sinner, and then He gives you the
strength and the power to turn from your sins. [422

...**Presence of Christ.** Today the person of Christ is
hidden from view, though His presence through the Holy
Spirit is in our hearts. Today is the day of faith. In "that
day," He will be revealed to our sight.   [423

97

...Sin. Sin shall no longer rule or dominate you when you are allowing the Holy Spirit to live Christ's life through you. [424

...Temptation. When you come to know Christ, there dwells within you the Holy Spirit, who gives you supernatural strength to overcome temptation and evil, so that when you face it, you don't face it alone. The Spirit of God gives you the power to say no. [425

HOME

A home is like a solar system. The center, the great sun, holds the solar system together. If it were not for the sun, the solar system would fly to pieces. Unless the Son of God is put at the center of your home, it, too, may fly to pieces. Make the Son of God the center of your home. [426

...Attitude Toward. I once read a statement by a certain lady. She said, "Why do I need a home? I was born in a hospital, educated in college, courted in an automobile, married in a church. I live out of a delicatessen—tin cans and paper bags. I spend my mornings on the golf course, my afternoons at the bridge table and my evenings at the movies. And when I die, I will be cremated and buried in a brass urn. All I really need is a garage." [427

...Christian. The word home is distinctively a holy word. It is so uniquely Christian that the language and dialects of heathen tongues do not contain its equivalent. It is part and parcel of the Christian faith. [428

Living creatively for Christ in the home is the acid test for any Christian man or woman. It is far easier to live an excellent life among your friends, when you are putting your best foot forward and are conscious of public opinion, than it is to live for Christ in your home.   [429

...Civilization. The foundations of civilization are no stronger and no more enduring than the corporate integrity of the homes on which they rest. If the home deteriorates, civilization will crumble and fall.   [430

...Disintegration. The disintegration of the American home is of great concern of all. The sociologist has made his study and has found out that some cancer is eating away at the vitals of the home. He thinks he knows what the problem is, but has not found a solution. Just so, the marriage counselor has taken advantage of an existing condition and has made his fortune on the misfortunes of frustrated couples. Even writers of columns to the lovelorn have suggestions and recommendations, but the problems continue, as they will continue until religion and Christ become the center of every home.   [431

...Example. I want to set an example in my home. I want my family to see Christ in me. If you will not live a godly life, if you will not be a God-fearing man for your own sake, then be a God-fearing man for your children's sake.   [432

...Foundation. The foundation upon which any happy home is built is the trust and affection a man has for his wife and the high regard in which she holds her husband. [433

...**Marriage.** The Supreme Court of the United States declared some time ago that "marriage is an institution, in the maintenance of which in its purity, the public is deeply interested, for it is the foundation of the family and of society, without which there would be neither civilization nor progress," and that "any trend or system which attacks the home condemns itself as hostile to public and personal welfare." [434

...**Religion.** In the early days there were no churches, no Sunday Schools, no public preaching. The only religion was in the home. Today, with all these opportunities for public worship, the father is still responsible for home training. [435

...**Unhappiness.** The basic reason for unhappiness in the home is the fact that we have disregarded God and the principles He has given us. We have refused to acknowledge His plan for the family. The members of the home have refused to accept their particular responsibilities as given in the Bible. [436

HONESTY

Honesty was once the hallmark of character. It has been set aside with an "It's all right if you don't get caught" philosophy. Only when we are in court are we required to tell the truth, the whole truth, and nothing but the truth. [437

HOPELESSNESS

Today there is a hopelessness and a pessimism in the air not felt by any previous generation. [438

HUMAN NATURE

Human nature is worst when conditions are best, and best when conditions are worst. [439

... Modern Man. What causes school children to attack teachers? . . . What causes bombs to be thrown against innocent people? . . . We must begin to realize that something is desperately wrong with human nature . . . We are afflicted with heart trouble. [440

HUMILITY

No man will ever be in heaven that has not humbled himself at the foot of the Cross of Christ. [441

HUSBAND

... Duty Of. Let us consider the duty of a husband in the home. Husband is an Anglo-Saxon word which means "the band of the house," or "the master of the house," the one who organizes it and holds it together and controls it. The wife is his chief assistant in this work. Just as all our duties to God and man are summed up in the word "love," so all the duties which the husband owes the wife are summed up in the command, "love your wife." [442

... Fidelity. A husband must be faithful to his wife. A man who is unfaithful to his wife in thought, word or deed has committed one of the greatest crimes known to God and man. It is one of the few sins for which God demanded the death penalty in the Old Testament. God says that no adulterer will be found in the kingdom of heaven. The wrath of God is waiting at the judgment day for any man who is unfaithful to his wife and guilty of this terrible sin. If you have committed this sin, renounce it, and then confess it to God. [443

...**Religious Responsibility.** A husband has the responsibility of leading the religious instruction in the home. The oldest and most important church in the world is the church of the household. The husband is the divinely ordained minister of that church. If you are not discharging the duty of leading your family in worship, then you are failing both God and them. You are putting your family in jeopardy. Any man who refuses to lead in devotions in his own home is dealing unjustly with his family and committing a crime against God. [444

· · I · ·

IDEOLOGIES

A war of ideologies is being waged throughout the world; a war of the secular against the spiritual. [445

IMMORALITY

... **Appearance.** Immorality, which is the sin of perversion and unnaturalness, has a way of making those who harbor it unnatural appearing. The shifty eye, the embarrassed blush, the suggestive glance—these are all marks of the impure. [446

... **Cure.** A medical doctor accepted Christ in one of our first Crusades. Before his conversion he was ruled by animal passion and was dedicated to a life of unchasity. His reading room was crammed full of salacious and suggestive literature and photographs. But after his conversion he was repulsed by the thought of impure practices and promptly gathered up all his lewd literature, carried it to a bridge and cast it into the river. Having experienced the new birth, he yielded himself to a new Master—Christ. He became one of the most active Christian laymen in the city and everyone respects him. [447

...Idleness. Idleness is one of the biggest contributing factors to immorality. [448

...Imagination. Man can commit immorality by evil imaginations. [449

...Marriage. If you commit immorality before marriage, a senior psychiatrist at Harvard University says it affects your marriage later. It affects all marriages later. There are no exceptions. [450

The sin of immorality is so terrible in the sight of God that it is the only thing that He allows to break the marriage relationship. Woe unto you that are guilty of this sin! Unless you confess your sins and forsake them, it would be better had you never been born! [451

...Modern Attitude. We have become so accustomed to immorality that it no longer seems to us to be immoral. [452

...National Security. The security of America is not being threatened by communism abroad so much as by immorality at home. [453

...Pre-Marital Affairs. We are being told by sociological statisticians that the majority of men and women have had affairs before marriage. [454

One of the best ways to get a boy to say "I do" at the marriage altar is for the girl to say "No" before marriage.[455

...Punishment; Historical. With immorality on the increase and with the divorce rate mounting, it is time that we take a long look at history. Under Jewish law, immorality was punishable by death. Under the Roman law it was punishable by death. Under the Greek law it was punishable by death. Under modern American law, of course, it is not punishable by death. But under God's law, its end is still death—spiritual death.   [456

...Sin. The sin of immorality is one of hell's keenest weapons for the destruction of souls, and satan has used it effectively from the dawn of creation to this present hour.   [457

IMMORTALITY

The Bible teaches that living inside of the body is the real you. You're a real person and that's the part of you that lives forever. Your body is going to go to the grave—but you, the real you—your intelligence, your memory, your personality —is going to live forever and ever. You never die and you're going to spend a million years, a billion years in one or two places, according to Jesus—not according to Billy Graham, but according to Jesus. Jesus talked a great deal about heaven, but He said three times more about hell than He did heaven.   [458

...Hope. However uncertain and vague the concept of immortality may be to multitudes of people, it has nevertheless always been mortal man's hope.   [459

...Job. Job, in the Old Testament, is the oldest book in the world. And Job asks the question that I'm sure disturbs many of you. He asks a question that every great philosopher has wrestled with. He asks a question that every great thinker and intellectual sometime wrestles with. He asks the same question that our greatest scientists ask. But neither philosophy nor science knows anything about it. That question is: If a man die, shall he live again? And the answer is a resounding YES! Yes, based on faith, the Word of God and Jesus' love for us.   [460

... **Salvation.** The Bible says we are dead in trespasses and in sins. There's no hope for your salvation. You see, you are going to live forever whether you like it or not. You don't have any choice in the matter; you can go out and blow your brains out but that's not going to change anything. Your soul, your spirit, your mind, the real you is going to live on and on, according to the Bible. You're destined to live for eternity. But where you spend your eternity is decided by Jesus Christ. The Bible says your spirit is lifeless, it's dead until God injects His life into your soul and that takes place the moment you receive Christ as your Lord and Savior.[461

... **Science.** It would seem that science is now in the process of trying to give to humanity a vague promise of immortality based upon chemical changes and formulas.[462

IMPURITY

... **Appearance.** The sin of impurity at the outset does not appear ugly and venomous. It comes in the guise of beauty, symmetry and desirability. There is nothing repulsive about it. Satan clothes his goddess of lust as an angel of

love, and her appearance has deceived the strongest of
men. [463

. . . Consequences Of. Some of the most miserable men I
know are those who are haunted by the memory of the
wasted, wanton years of impurity. God is willing to forgive
them, but they are not willing to forgive themselves. [464

. . . Human Love. Impurity is one of the most revolting of
sins, because it twists and distorts one of God's most precious
gifts to man—human love, and drags it down to the level of
the beast. [464-A

. . . Sin. The sin of impurity has caused nations to fall. It
has over and over again ruined the sanctity of the home. It
has hindered the health and development of the personality,
and it has caused the spiritual impotence of thousands. It
has filled our divorce courts, made thousands of innocent
children homeless and has wrecked the hope of the bright to-
morrow for many a young person. [465

INCARNATION

Man, fettered and bound, was incapable of coming to
God, so God, in love and mercy, came down to earth to
consort with men. The creature could not come up to God,
so the Creator condescended to come down to redeem His
creation. [466

. . . History. Christ's coming in the flesh—His invading
the world—His identifying Himself with sinful man—is the
most significant fact in all history. [467

INDIFFERENCE

The greatest public enemy is not the Mafia or communism—it is indifference! [468

INGRATITUDE

One of the worst sins that we can commit is that of ingratitude. [469

INIQUITY

The mystery of iniquity is the power unseen, unknown except by its effects, which is ever working in the world for evil. [470

INQUIRY

We could not discourage the honest inquirer. Rather, we would welcome him. [471

INSECURITY

Why live in insecurity and lack of assurance when it is not necessary? The Apostle Paul, writing to the Philippians, told them to "rejoice." He used the word "joy" many times, yet he was in jail in Rome at the time. [472

INSINCERITY

The world has been offended by our insincerity. The world has been misled by our insincerity. The world has been discouraged by our insincerity. This is the greatest stumbling block to evangelism in the world today. [473

INTEGRATION

Full integration will come quicker in the South than in the North, because down there, we are kin to each other.   [474

... **Bible.** There is nothing in the Bible to forbid inter-marriage.   [475

INTEGRITY

On a drive through the Swiss countryside in 1962, I was asked by a friend, "What do you consider the most important thing in life?" "Integrity," I answered. "Suppose," he said, "you could choose between a billion dollar gift to spend for Christian causes; Russia's leaders' conversion to Jesus Christ; or an open door to evangelize the entire communist world—which would you take?" "Still integrity!" I insisted.   [476

... **America.** Today's political leaders point out the moral ills of America, but none of them seem to have an answer to the desperate need for a new moral integrity that would reverse the moral plunge that Americans are now taking.   [477

INTELLECT

... **Emotion; Will.** There are three little men that live down inside of every one of us. One is intellect, another is emotion, and the third is will. Intellectually, you may accept Christ. Emotionally, you may feel that you can love Him. However, until you have surrendered to Christ by a definite act of your will, you are not a Christian.   [478

. . . The Gospel. The gospel provides for man's intellect. It stimulates his intellect to the highest activity. It commands the complete education of all his intellectual powers. [479

INTOLERANCE

. . . Christ. Christ was so intolerant of man's lost estate that He left His lofty throne in the heavens, took on Himself the form of man, suffered at the hands of evil men and died a shameful death on a cruel cross to purchase our redemption. Having paid such a price, He could not be tolerant about man's indifference toward Him and the redemption He has wrought. [480

. . . Hypocrisy. Jesus was intolerant toward hypocrisy. He pronounced more "woes" on the Pharisees than on any other group because they were given to outward piety, but inward sham. [481

INTROSPECTION

There is an outward you and there's an inward you. And you never really see the inward you unless you let Christ help you look inside your heart. Through acceptance of Him and meditation in His word, He will lead you to self-understanding. [482

INVOLVEMENT

In the face of social evil, neutrality is not Christian. Whether we like it or not, we are involved—for better or for worse. [483

· · J · ·

JEALOUSY

...**Christ.** The Pharisees and Sadducees were jealous of the attention that Christ received. They were envious of the great crowds that flocked to hear Him, and because the people had made somewhat of a hero of Christ. Their jealousy burned as flames of fire in their hearts and caused them to scheme to put Him to death.　　　[484

...**Home.** Jealousy provokes suspicion and, finally, that green-eyed monster will wreck a home and throw the children upon the mercy of a society that already has too many problems.　　　[485

...**Marriage.** Jealousy is an enemy of the home. It is the failure of one or the other to trust his partner.　[486

JESUS

...**Door To Heaven.** There are many ways that look appealing and alluring, but there is but one door to heaven and that one door can be opened only by Jesus. [487

. . . Faith In.   No man has sins forgiven, no man goes to heaven, no man has assurance of peace and happiness, until he has faith in Jesus.   [488

. . . God.   Jesus and the living God go together. There is no such thing as a Jesus Gospel. The Gospel is the news of the redemptive working of God in and through Jesus Christ.   [489

. . . Love.   No man ever loved like Jesus. He taught the blind to see and the dumb to speak. He died on the cross to save us. He bore our sins. And now God says, "Because He did, I can forgive you."   [490

. . . Son Of God.   When Jesus, the Son of God, came to the world, He declared the importance of His partnership with God when He said: "I must be about my Father's business."   [491

. . . The World's Hope.   Jesus Christ is the hope of the world. There is no possibility that the nations of the world will ever solve the basic problems of human nature until Christ comes again.   [492

JUDGMENT

. . . Certainty.   The Bible says there is no possible way of escape. Sooner or later we must leave our dream world and face up to the fact of God, sin and judgment.   [493

. . . Completeness.   Jesus said every secret thing will be brought out at the judgment. Nothing will be hidden. [494

... Individuals. The Bible says we are going to be judged one by one. You are not going to be there with a big crowd of people; you are going to be all by yourself.   [495

... Life And Death. Too many Christians try to put off the thought of death and of the fact that all children of God will one day stand before the judgment seat of Christ to give an account of how they spent their time here on earth. [496

... Loneliness. You may be one of a crowd now, but the day is coming when each one of you must stand alone before Almighty God and be judged. That will be for you the climax of all the loneliness of earth, and the preview of the loneliness of hell.   [497

... Modern Man. The very goodness of God should drive us to Jesus Christ, but instead we have followed the materialism of our times and maybe—maybe, God may allow judgment to come in order to drive us to the cross in repentance and plea for forgiveness.   [498

... Nearness. The wheels of God's judgment can be heard by discerning souls across the length and breadth of nations. Things are happening fast! The need for a return to God has never been more urgent.   [499

JUSTICE

... Judgment. God does not judge men by a monetary standard. He weighs them upon the scales of justice and integrity.   [500

JUVENILE DELINQUENCY

... **Causes.** There is no single cause of delinquency, but certainly one cause is a feeling of insecurity on the part of young offenders. Among the factors contributing to insecurity are poverty, liquor in the home, father coming home drunk, strained relationships between parents, often accompanied by harsh language and quarrels in the presence of the children—all these things generate fear and help to lay the foundations for later crime. Many children are insecure because they are not loved.   [501

··K··

KINGDOM OF GOD

There are no short cuts to the Kingdom of God.   [502

KINGDOM OF HEAVEN

...**Entry.** Jesus said except you come as little children and be converted, you cannot enter the kingdom of heaven.   [503

KNOWLEDGE

We are teaching thousands of young people in this country knowledge; but we are not helping them to know how to use that knowledge.   [504

...**Wisdom.** The Bible warns not to confuse knowledge with wisdom. Knowledge is horizontal. Wisdom is vertical—it comes down from above.   [505

·•L•·

LATIN AMERICA

...**Communism.** In Latin America, thousands formerly disposed toward Christianity are turning in desperation to communism.   [506

LAW

...**America.** Today law and order are breaking down in the United States. In some areas there is almost a state of anarchy.   [507

...**Church And State.** We are entering a dangerous period when we deny prayers in the school or refuse to allow the singing of the fourth verse of "America" or say a county commission can't place a lighted cross on the side of a courthouse.   [508

...**Definition.** The law is a moral mirror. It condemns, but does not convert.   [509

...**Limitations.** Law can elevate society, but it cannot reach the principles from which our behavior springs. [510

...**Man.** The trouble with people nowadays is that everyone wants to be a law unto himself. [511

...**Necessity.** We must have laws; we must have discipline. Otherwise society can become chaotic. [512

...**Sin.** The law deals with the effects of sin, but Christ deals with sin's causes. [513

...**Supreme Court.** The Supreme Court is going to have to clarify its rulings on the separation of Church and State. [514

The Supreme Court, in trying to protect freedom, is giving the nation dangerous license. [515

...**World.** Ours is a world of violence, where lawlessness and crime prevail. [516

LAZINESS

Many a man has lost his life in an automobile accident, not because he was a bad driver, but because he was asleep at the wheel. Many persons are fighting losing battles spiritually, not because they are really bad, but because they are spiritually lazy, sleepy and drowsy. [517

...**Spiritual Purpose.** The worst thing that laziness does is to rob a man of spiritual purpose—the power of Christian decision. [518

117

LIFE

... Brevity. Though you live to be 70, 80, or 90 years old, that is but a snap of the finger compared to eternity. Therefore we should all be aware of the brevity of this life and the necessity for preparing ourselves for eternity. [519

... Emphasis. Undue emphasis upon the importance of the body has created a system of thought which is more concerned with the accommodations of life's journey than with its destination. [520

... Escapism. There are many of you who, instead of facing up to the realities of sin and defeat in life, are trying to hide in an illusive, imaginary world. But the Bible warns there is no possible way of escape. Sooner or later we must leave our dream world and face up to the facts of God, of sin and of judgment. [521

... God And Man. The Bible reveals that God has a plan for every life, and that if we live in constant fellowship with Him, He will direct and lead us in the fulfillment of this plan. [522

... Long View Of. I beg you not to squander life. I beseech you to take the long view. Do not live for this world only. [523

... Point Of Living. We live in this world, that is true. But the point of living is: Don't be subdued by it. [524

. . . Preparation For Eternity. Are you prepared? The Bible says, "These things I write unto you that believe on the son of God that ye know that you have eternal life." I can therefore say to you, with the authority of this Book, that I know my sins are forgiven. I know I'm going to heaven, to have life as long as God lives—forever. If life everlasting is what you seek, then you must prepare in this life for it.   [525

. . . Sacrifice. Our ability to contribute to life is dependent upon ability to suffer and sacrifice.   [526

. . . Satisfaction. If Isaiah lived today he would probably stand on a street corner in New York, or Chicago or on Market Street in San Francisco, and simply ask the milling, restless throngs: "Are you getting what you want? Are you finding satisfaction?" He would say to the actress, surfeited with fame and fortune who peers out on life hungrily: "Are you getting what you want?" He would say to the successful financier who commands his fleets and controls his industries: "Are you getting what you want?" He would say to the laborers and workmen of America who are enjoying the highest standard of living in history: "Are you getting what you want?" He would say to the youth of America who dance and go-go, "Are you getting what you want?" He would say to the consumers of America who have the best homes, the most comfortable furniture, the finest food, the most clever gadgets, and the smoothest, most powerful automobiles: "Are you really getting what you want?" And Isaiah would not leave them with the question unanswered.

He would tell them: "There is a satisfying way of life—if only you will seek it." [527

...**Span.** If you've lived beyond 70 years of age, you're living on extended grace and mercy, according to the Bible. A hundred years from now the three billion people who are now living on the earth will all be dead—and a hundred years is only a moment in eternity. [528

...**Ways.** There are not many ways of life, just two: the right way and the wrong way. [529

LONELINESS

...**Christian.** Perhaps there is no loneliness quite so bitter as the loneliness of a backslidden Christian. [530

...**Man.** Did you ever watch the people coming out of a night club or leaving a casino? There are few smiles as a rule, and most faces are as grim as when they went in. They are lost and lonely, even in the midst of the crowd. [531

...**Sin.** There are thousands of lonely people in the city and in the country, who carry heavy and difficult burdens of grief, anxiety, pain and disappointment; but the loneliest soul of all is the man whose life is steeped in sin. [532

LOVE

True love is always costly. [533

...**Action.** There is a sense in which true love is a fire. Genuine love can never be complacent and passive. It is the man who loves his school most who shouts the loudest for his team at a football game.   [534

   ... **Advice On.**   I remember that two or three times I thought I was in love. They called it puppy love, but it was real to the puppy! I remember that one day I decided that I was going to wait on God. I didn't know that way out in China, God was preparing a lovely young woman just for me. She was the right one in temperament and in her experience. She had to leave her home when she was thirteen to go to school in Korea. She said she never dreamed that God was preparing her for a lifetime of good-byes. God specially prepared Ruth to be my wife for this particular ministry that He called me to. God has someone chosen just for you. Wait on God. Get God's man, God's woman; and there will be little danger of a breakup of your marriage.   [535

   ... **Christian.**   It seems that love is the real key to Christian unity. In the spirit of true humility, compassion, consideration and unselfishness, which reflect the mind of the Lord Jesus, we are to approach our problems, our work and even our differences.   [536

   ... **Cost Of.**   True love is never cheap. And the proof of love is its capacity to suffer for the object of its affection. [537

   ... **Destructive.**   To preserve some things, love must destroy others. It is never neutral!   [538

...Enemies. When you come to Jesus Christ and accept Him as your Lord and Savior, He gives you a supernatural love that allows you to love your enemy whom you normally would not love. [539

...Free. The advocates of free love and the interpreters of Freud have left their mark on society. We are a nation that trembles with fear at the threat of universal destruction, but we refuse to turn from our great national sins. [540

...God. Whatever you love most, be it sports, pleasure, business or God, that is your god! [541

...God's Love Of Man. God loves you. You're rebellious, you cheat, you commit immorality, you're selfish, you sin, but God loves you with an intensity beyond anything that I could describe to you. He loves you, and He loves you so much that He gave His only son Jesus Christ to die on that cross and the thing that kept Christ on that cross was love, not the nail. [542

...Home. The first essential in a happy Christian home is that love must be practiced. [543

...Hypocrisy. There are those today who speak glibly of "love" and under the guise of the Gospel breathe out their slanders, lies and the spirit of envy. [544

...Jesus. No man ever loved like Jesus. He made the blind to see and the deaf to hear and the dumb to speak. He fed the hungry. He said to all those who get tired working, "Come unto me, all of you that labor and are heavy laden and I'll give you rest." I could put my confidence in a person like that.   [545

... Marriage. I don't believe a man and a woman can really love each other outside of Christ. I believe that Christ gives a new depth—to married love. A new dimension of love. He can rekindle the love of your heart.   [546

... Power Of. If you have love, you are not only going to think no evil, you're going to take your tongue and have it nailed to the cross so that you bless instead of curse.   [547

... Race Relations. There is not a person who has the ability to love as he should unless he first loves Christ and the Holy Spirit has control of his life. That's the reason for the race problem in America today. We have legislation, and we need legislation, but it will be nothing but a cold war unless the love of God is in our hearts. That's the reason we must have a spiritual revival in our country—to save it. Men who turn to God love their neighbor no matter what the color of his skin, no matter what his circumstances. This is the love that God gives as a gift, and it is produced in the heart by the Holy Spirit who lives there.   [548

... Reciprocity. Love is also reciprocal. Unless there is a human response to divine love, unless we can say, "I live by the faith of the Son of God, who loved me, and gave Himself for me," we have not entered into a love pact.   [549

...Theology. It is possible to be right theologically and yet to be lacking in a spirit of love, which is exactly the condition of the demons. [550

...True. It is the man who loves his neighbor most who will fight against all that hurts, deprives and oppresses his neighbor. [551

LYING

The Christian must avoid lying and distrust those who practice it. [552

...Conscience. Now the conscience, the Bible teaches us, can be hardened. It can be deadened. The first time that a man tells a straight-out, deliberate lie his conscience may bother him for days. But he can go on and become a habitual liar until, after a while, he can tell a lie and his conscience doesn't bother him. [553

· • M · ·

MAN

... **Associations.** Man should know that Jesus wasn't afraid to associate with anyone!   [554

... **Capacity.** Man is a little creature with a big capacity, a finite being with infinite desires, deserving nothing but demanding all. God made man with his huge capacity and desire in order that He might come in and completely satisfy that desire.   [555

... **Destinies.** There are two destinies—heaven and hell. You have to decide which one you want to spend eternity in. He said there are two roads—the narrow road and the broad road. You have to decide. He said one leads to destruction; the other, to eternal life.   [556

... **Divided.** Man without God is always torn between two urges. His nature prompts him to do wrong, and his conscience urges him to do right.   [557

... **Foes.** Man has three foes: the world, the flesh and the devil. The attitude of the Christian to all three of them is summed up in one word—renounce.   [558

. . . Free Will. God did not create man to be a puppet or a robot. He gave us a will of our own, so that we can live any way we want to. We can accept or reject God, that is our privilege, for we were made in His image.   [559

Man, of his own free will, went away from God. He must, by deliberate choice, come back to God. God has done all that needs to be done as far as His part of the transaction is concerned; but there is one thing that He cannot touch: your will. He cannot force you to accept the life He holds out to you.   [560

. . . Future. We must not dwell on what man has been or what man is; we must think of what he can be by the grace of God. Because of what Christ did on the Cross, we can be reconciled to God.   [561

. . . God's Love. God created man because God loves and wanted an object to love. He created man so that he could return His love.   [562

. . . Head Of The Home. In one sense, the husband and wife are co-equal in the home; but when it comes to the governmental arrangement of the family, the Bible, from Genesis to Revelation, teaches that man is to be the head of the home. We have many women today in America who are wearing the trousers in the family. Some of them have to, because they have married the type of man who refuses to take his proper responsibility in the home. But the principle the Bible teaches is that the husband be the head of the house.   [563

...**Ideals.** All mankind is searching for ideal conditions in a world that is anything but ideal.   [564

...**Inadequacy.** Experience reveals that we are inadequate. History proves that man is inadequate. The Bible declares that you are inadequate to save yourself. Christ's coming to the world proves the inadequacy of the race. [565

...**Modern.** Man today cannot understand the deepseated sickness of the human race, nor does he have any clue to the cure. So he stumbles and gropes from crisis-tocrisis, completely blind as to the real nature of the disease.   [566

We are slaves to our gadgets, puppets of our power, and prisoners of our security. The theme of our generation is: "Get more, know more, and do more," instead of "Pray more, be more, and serve more."   [567

...**New Awakening.** The young man who turns his interest from "hot rods" to college and sees the need for learning; the alcoholic who realizes his plight and starts back on the trail to sobriety and decency; the community ne'er-dowell who turns and tries to make a man of himself—these all experience a certain kind of new awakening.   [568

...**Paradox Of.** Most thoughtful people recognize that man is a paradox. He is both dust of earth and breath of God. He is a contradiction of discord and harmony, hatred and love, pride and humility, tolerance and intolerance, and peace and turmoil. The depths to which he sinks only dramatize the heights to which, by God's grace, he is capable of rising. [569

... **Prayer.** Man instinctively prays. He begins in childhood with: "Now I lay me down to sleep," and when life's burdens oppress, he prays with groanings that cannot be uttered. [570

... **Separated From God.** A hungry man is a dangerous man, and a man away from God can be expected to be plagued by phobias, fears and complexes. [571

... **Sin.** The Bible teaches that man's soul is already lost through sin. The only thing that can be done is to acknowledge that you are a sinner, and put your faith in Jesus Christ, accepting Him as your personal Savior. [572

... **Without God.** Man without God is a contradiction and a monstrosity. [573

MANAGEMENT

... **Labor.** If Christ's words prevailed in labor-management relations, there would be no strikes; management would treat employees with generosity; employees would be eager to put in a full day's work for their hire because they would not only be working for their wages, they would be working for God. [574

MARRIAGE

... **Adultery.** The Bible reveals how God safeguards the

marriage relationship by imposing the strictest penalties on adultery and fornication. [575

... **Bible.** It is high time that our so-called experts on marriage, the family, and the home, turn to the Bible. We have read newspaper columns and listened to counselors on the radio; psychiatrists have had a land-office business. In it all, the One who performed the first marriage in the Garden of Eden and instituted the union between man and wife has been left out. [576

... **Christian.** I would not guarantee that with becoming a Christian, the whole problem of marriage and the home is automatically solved. But I do say that complete fulfillment in marriage can never be realized outside of the life in Christ. [577

... **Courtship.** If couples would put half the effort into marriage that they put into courtship, they would be surprised how things will brighten up. [578

... **Disrespect.** We are finding that disrespect for each other before marriage cannot change to respect after marriage. Love is not lust, and lust is not love. Love, if it is anything at all, is respect; and when respect for the other's dignity and integrity is thrown aside, love folds up like a punctured balloon. [579

... **Divine.** Marriage is a divine institution. Society did not make the first marriage; it was founded by God. God made marriage. [580

...Divorce. Marriage is a lifelong relationship. It is not right that a husband or wife should be changed for another according to the wishes of either. In the marriage vows, it is always read: "What God has joined together, let no man separate." But our culture no longer frowns upon the exchange of a mate. [581

The Bible teaches that marriage can terminate in only one way without provoking God's displeasure. That way is indicated in the marriage pledge promising faithfulness "until death do you part." [582

...Reasons. Some get married out of a feeling of insecurity, some because of inferiorities, some out of loneliness, some out of a desire for escape from the realities of life, some out of sexual passion, some out of spite, some to gain social prestige. I heard about one boy that flipped a coin, saying, "Shall I get married, or not?" It came down heads, and he said, "Yes, I'll get married." No wonder his marriage broke up six weeks later. [583

...Religion. I would advise every couple planning to establish a home to first come to a complete agreement on their religious faith. [584

MATERIALISM

A moral and political erosion is taking place around the world as false ideologies of materialism are gaining ground. [585

The things which materialism offers cannot satisfy the innermost longings of the human heart, nor can materialism save us when the showdown comes, as surely it must. [586

... Reason For. Materialism is growing because we have tried to get Christ to abdicate from the realms of politics, economics, science and education. [587

... Things, The Best Are Free. The best things in life are free, are they not? The air we breathe is not sold by the cubic foot. The water which flows crystal clear from the mountain stream is free for the taking. Love is free, faith is free, hope is free. [588

MERCY

... Jesus. Jesus stopped dying on the cross long enough to answer the prayer of a thief. He stopped in a big crowd one day because someone touched the hem of His garment; and He'll stop to touch your life and change you, and forgive you. He knows you by name. He has the hairs of your head numbered. He has your name written in His books and everything that you have done from the time you were born to this hour. All the secret things, all the private things, they are all there. He knows all about you and He loves you. He says He'll forgive you if you will put your trust and your confidence in Him. [589

... Justice. I've heard some people say they want justice. But I don't want justice—for if I have justice, I'm lost. I don't deserve heaven. I don't deserve to be forgiven. I am a sinner, I deserve to be lost. I deserve to go to hell. I want mercy. I want the grace of God and I'm glad to read in the Bible that God is the God of love. And God is not willing that any should perish, but that all should have eternal life. He loves me, no matter what my sins and He offers me mercy, grace and forgiveness. [590

METHODIST CHURCH

I have read the journals of George Whitefield and the journals of John Wesley, and I'm convinced that George Whitefield has as much to do with the founding of the Methodist Church as John Wesley. [591

MILITARY POWER

We must have military power to keep madmen from taking over the world. [592

MIND

Your mind should become the mind of the resurrected Christ—to think His thoughts. It should become the very mind of Christ, because He thinks through you. And this can happen when you let Christ have your mind and body and life for His purposes. [593

MINORITY

...Power Of. According to the historical record, it doesn't take a lot of people to change the trend of events. A few people who know what they believe, and are not afraid to express it, can change the world. [594

MISERY

Poor, frustrated, deluded souls run like frightened beasts

into the jungle of worldly pleasure, only to emerge more miserable than before. [595

MISSIONS

Through the centuries, the Church of Jesus Christ has flourished in exact ratio to its interest in missions. [596

MISUNDERSTANDING

...Christian Experience. The dreadful uncertainty that haunts the souls of many persons grows out of a misunderstanding of what the Christian experience is. [597

MODERN LIFE

Never before in the history of the world have men been faced with the tremendous and overwhelming problems that face us today. And never before have we possessed weapons that could destroy such vast areas of civilization as the weapons we have today. [598

MONEY

...A Trust. All our money is only a trust, and we are stewards of that trust. [599

...Attitude. If a person gets his attitude toward money straight, it will help straighten out almost every other area of his life. [600

...God. Tell me what you think about money, and I can tell you what you think about God, for these two are closely related. A man's heart is closer to his wallet than almost anything else. [601

...Heaven. Jesus said that money could be so great a temptation that it would be a stumbling block to the kingdom of heaven. [602

...Importance. Think of the things that cannot be bought with money. It cannot buy health, friends, love, or peace of heart and mind. It cannot buy peace of soul. We come to the conclusion then, that money in itself is not worthy of the importance most people place upon it. [603

...Jesus' Words. Our standard of living in America is the highest in the world. By many standards we are all rich, and Jesus said it's hard for a rich man to enter into heaven. Jesus talked a great deal about money and the problems it causes man—in fact, one-fifth of all Jesus had to say was about money. [604

...Love Of. The making of money is necessary for daily living, but money-making is apt to degenerate into money-loving, and then the deceitfulness of riches enters in and spoils our spiritual life. [605

...Use Of. Money is a gift of God and it is to be used for His glory. If it is squandered selfishly, or employed greedily, it cankers and brings misery and distress upon him who possesses it. [606

MORALITY

...America. The strength of the nation and its capacity to carry out its responsibilities in the world, or even to survive, depends upon the moral strength of the nation.

Other nations will not respect us for very long as a people if we have lost respect for ourselves. [607

What is happening in America? Where is our sense of moral values? Have we, as a people, sunk so low that the only persons we are interested in reading about and seeing are the harlots and adulterers? No wonder the American home is crumbling. [608

... **Behavior.** We have changed our moral code to fit our behavior instead of changing our behavior to harmonize with our moral code. [609

... **Christian Ideals.** Under the guise of liberty and free thinking, the Christian ideals of chastity and fidelity are attacked as outmoded, narrow-minded Puritanism. [610

... **Intellectuals.** Thousands of so-called intellectuals have publicly stated that morality is relative, that there is no norm or absolute. In this, I do not blame our young people so much as I blame those who are guilty of contributing to the inflaming of their passions. [611

... **"Low Living."** We all know that the high cost of "low living" is leading to moral bankruptcy, but we lack the moral strength to resist. [612

... **National Security.** The moral problem of our nation has become so serious that it threatens the very security of the nation. [613

MORAL PROGRESS

One of the reasons that our moral progress has not kept pace with our scientific progress is that we have, as a people, rejected one of the most effective means of moral progress, the spiritual revival. [614

MORALS

... **Bible.** According to the Bible, God's moral demands are not relative—they are absolute and unchangeable. [615

... **Instruction.** Man needs moral and religious instructions as much as he needs scientific and cultural instructions. [616

... **Mores.** I am more concerned with mini-morals than I am with mini-skirts. [617

... **"Wild Oats."** Many "nervous breakdowns" can be traced to the loose morals of college years. "Wild oats" have a way of hounding people through the years and springing up at most embarassing moments. [618

MOTHERS

... **Christian.** Only God Himself fully appreciates the influence of a Christian mother in the molding of the character in her children . . . If we had more Christian mothers we would have less delinquency, less immorality, less ungodliness and fewer broken homes. The influence of a mother in her home upon the lives of her children cannot be measured. They know and absorb her example and attitudes when it comes to questions of honesty, temperance, kindness and industry . . . [619

...Prayer. A man who has a praying mother has a most cherished possession. I can think of no greater heritage than that of a saintly, praying mother. I have thanked God over and over again for a Christian mother. [620

...Responsibility. Every mother owes it to her children to accept Christ as her personal Savior, that she may be the influence for good in the lives of those whom Christ has graciously given to her. [621

MYSTERY

A "mystery" in Scripture is a previously hidden truth now divinely revealed, but in which there is still a supernatural element that remains unknown despite the revelation. [622

...Skepticism. The most common objection to the new birth is caused by the element of mystery. "How can these things be?" the student asks. Or, "How can I believe in something I don't understand?" It is natural for the student to think in the framework of textbooks and test tubes, but he should know that not all of life is confined to books and test tubes, to formulas and equations. [623

· · N · ·

NARROWNESS

... **The Narrow Road.** Science is narrow and exacting. Mathematical laws are narrow. Chemical laws are narrow. Jesus said the road to heaven was narrow, and He laid it out just as specifically as you lay out the multiplication table. Some of you say, "I'll get there, but I'll make my own rules; I'll go my own way; I'll do good unto others. I'll try to live as good as I can." Jesus said to Nicodemus, "Nicodemus, that's not enough. You must be born again!" And you must follow the narrow road, within the narrow bounds of what Jesus taught. [624

... **Tolerance.** Some do not choose the narrow road, because they want to be tolerant. I think we've become far too tolerant of too many things. We are too tolerant of those people that are against the basic principles of this country. Jesus was tolerant of many things, but He was also narrow minded about many things. We should be intolerant of those things which Christ would not tolerate. [625

NATIONS

If ever there was an hour when all nations needed to turn to God in humility and confession of sin, it is now. [626

...Armed Might. Today our nation ranks with the greatest powers on the face of the earth. But if we put our trust in armed might instead of Almighty God, the coming conflict could conceivably go against us.   [627

...Future. Because the present is so black, I cannot see a bright future for the nations of the world unless there is an imminent turning to God, and it must begin with individuals.   [628

...God. No nation has ever fallen in the history of the world that was right with God.   [629

NEGLECT

Neglect of a man's spiritual life can take away his appetite for the righteous things of God.   [630

NEW BIRTH

The new birth which Jesus requires of every man is equally as important as your first birth.   [631

The new birth is not something you do for yourself. It is something that is done for you! Yours is the task of believing and receiving rather than comprehending and doing. [632

...Miracle. The new birth is a miracle of life. It is something we accept as real, but not comprehensible. Life is not so fully understood that we can pour it into tiny molds of our limited reason.   [633

...Necessity. Jesus said you'll never see the kingdom of heaven unless you are born again. This is not hereditary.

Sometime, somewhere you have got to cross the line. My children have a godly mother. They have a preacher for their father. But my children would be as lost as anybody else's children unless they personally themselves, sometime decide for Jesus Christ. They are not Christians because their father is a preacher. You cannot inherit it. It's not a physical change. It's a spiritual change. Something takes place down inside when God comes to live within. [634

THE "NEW MORALITY" MOVEMENT

We see ministers and atheists marching comfortably together and theologians preaching fervently that the secular world is not really evil—in spite of the fact that Jesus warned, "As the world hated me, so it will hate you also." In fact, to some of these men evil is no longer called evil. The so-called "new morality" also finds some clergymen engulfed in heated debate over the Christian attitude toward premarital sex and pornography. They have embarked upon a so-called "intellectual" effort that is contrary to the teachings of God and His holy word. For there is no "new morality"— there is only one morality—the morality taught by Jesus Christ. [635

NEW THEOLOGY

... **Dialectical Materialists.** Dialectical materialists don't even object to Christ on the cross. It is there that they would keep Him—dying, bleeding, incapacitated. They reject a risen, living Christ who would expose the falseness of their ideology and break into smithereens the empire they have built by subterfuge and deceit. [636

NON-CONFORMITY

Jesus calls you to be a non-conformist. Love not the world nor the things in the world, for if any man loves the world, the love of the Father is not in him. Live to be separated from the evils of the world. Live to be different. [637

... **Christianity.** A true Christian, living an obedient life, is a constant rebuke to those who accept the moral standards of this world. [638

OBEDIENCE

...Necessity Of. Only by a life of obedience to the voice of the Spirit, by a daily denying of self, by a full dedication to Christ and constant fellowship with Him, are we enabled to live a godly life and an influential life in this present ungodly world.   [639

...Trust. The Scripture teaches that a Christian is one who trusts Christ as his Savior and obeys Him as Lord. Trust gets him into the Kingdom, but obedience and love to God are the badges of citizenship.   [640

OMISSION

The unsurrendered Christian stands condemned for what he does not do more than for what he does.   [641

...Sins Of. The Bible teaches that possibly the greatest sins that can be committed are those of omission.   [642

OMNIPOTENCE

Amidst the world's confusion, God's omnipotent hand moves, working out His unchanging plan and purpose; and the kingdoms of this world shall become the Kingdom of the Lord Jesus Christ, "For He must reign till He hath put all enemies under His feet" (1 Corinthians 15:25).   [643

OPPRESSION

I feel it is my duty to warn the American people that a day of reckoning is coming. We cannot ignore the oppressed, suffering and helpless peoples behind the Iron Curtain without paying for it at the judgment of God. [644

ORGANIZATION

... **Churches.** We have so watered down the message of the Christ and are so interested in numbers, statistics, money and denominational organization and growth that we have lost the Gospel itself.   [645

ORGANIZED RELIGION

... **Rebellion Against.** Young people today are rebelling against religion. Not against Christ, not against God or true spiritual experience, but against organized Christianity, against the church.   [646

· · P · ·

PACIFISM

Pacifism will fail, for the pacifist acts as if all men are regenerate and can be appealed to through persuasion and goodwill. [647

PARENTS

... **Children.** For you who have children who have departed from God and are worried about them, I would suggest several things. First, a prayer of confession. Perhaps you failed in the home in the way you brought them up. Second, pray for them. Third, I would suggest that you live as an example before them. Let them see Christ in you. [648

... **Disrespect Of.** When you hear children speaking of their parents or to their parents disrespectfully, set them down as illbred and unmannerly children, however polished and polite they may be in company. [649

... **Failure.** Parents have communicated their own purposelessness and meaningless of life to their children. They have done wrong in failing to perform their chief function in life—that of making a home for their children. They provide everything but love. [650

...**Home Life.** Very seldom do parents have trouble with children when the Bible is read regularly in the home, grace is said at the table and family prayers take place daily. [651

...**Permissiveness.** A traveler from Europe visiting America said: "One unique thing about America is the way the parents obey their children." [652

...**Responsibilities.** Every child has the right to good parents. Every child has the right to be taught about God and moral law. Our children can be no better than the homes from which they come. [653

PARTNERSHIP

...**God And Man.** Some Christians have not learned that life is a partnership between God and man. Christ said: "Take my yoke upon you." When we are yoked with Christ, pulling as a team, life's burdens are easily borne. [654

PATRIOTISM

Today in America if you are a patriot, salute the flag, sing "The Star Spangled Banner,"and say you believe in America, you are immediately in conflict with those who are saying patriotism is passe. [655

PEACE

...**Deceit.** There is a reason that many of the peace

treaties which have been signed in human history have not been kept and war has ensued. These treaties have been signed in good faith, but they were signed on the basis of trusting the motives of the other party. They have been broken time after time and millions have died on the battle-fields of the world because the human heart is deceitful and desperately wicked. [656

... **False.** We have our peace movements, and all we want is peace-abroad and at home. But if by peace we mean appeasing tyranny, compromising with gangsters and being silent because we haven't the moral fortitude to speak out against injustice, then this is not real peace. It is a false peace. It is a farce and it is a hoax. [657

... **From God.** Peace is not arbitrary. It must be based upon definite facts. God has all the facts on His side; the world does not. Therefore God, and not the world, can give peace. [658

... **Peacemakers.** Peace-making is a noble vocation. But you can no more make peace in your own strength than a mason can build a wall without a trowel, a carpenter build a house without a hammer or an artist paint a picture without a brush. You must have the proper equipment. To be a peacemaker, you must know the Peace Giver. To make peace on earth, you must know the peace of heaven. You must know Him who "is our peace." [659

PEOPLE

The vast majority of the people around the world are

looking to politics, science and education for the solution of life's problems and not to Jesus Christ.   [660

...**Happiness.** I could tell you of many people who have explored every earthly resource for happiness and failed, but eventually came in repentance and faith to Christ and in Him found satisfaction.   [661

PERSONALITY

The word personality comes from a Latin word which means mask. There's many a beautiful face hiding a very miserable heart, a very bored heart.   [662

PHILANTHROPY

We should be philanthropic and give to charitable organizations that are doing good for the betterment of mankind.   [663

PHILOSOPHY

A well-known counselor on home and family relations obtained a divorce, confessing that his theories of marital happiness based on a humanistic philosophy had failed in his own experience—yet thousands had listened to his radio counsel for years. All across the nation hundreds of educators, counselors, psychiatrists and philosophers are finding out they don't have the answers and they are throwing up their hands and crying for help.   [664

...**Bible.** Christians must realize that a Bible-based philosophy of world events and world destiny will never parallel the world's philosophies. As Christians we are not obligated to attempt a reconciliation of the Bible's teachings to modern philosophies. [665

...**Religious Education.** Most of the philosophy of modern religious education has been based on the idea that a person can become a Christian by a process of education. This is not accurate. Becoming a Christian involves conversion, acceptance, surrender and faith. These cannot be taught as a part of philosophy and education. [666

...**Wrong Choices.** It is contrary to reason for a thirsty person to turn from a pure, sparkling mountain stream to quench his thirst at a stale, putrid cistern—yet that is what the human race does when it rejects God's truth and standards in favor of the Devil's impure philosophies. [667

PLEASURE

The river of pleasure, though it flows through lush meadows and beautiful glens, contains no healing for the soul. [668

...**Overuse.** Pleasure is legitimate in itself, but wrong if overused. For overuse is abuse. [669

...**Sinful.** Sinful pleasure will ruin your appetite for the things of God. [670

POLITICIANS

...**Peter; Matthew.** God took Peter—a zealot, a political reactionary of his day—and diverted his energy and his una-bounding enthusiasm to high purposes instead of low, and he helped lead a movement which reshaped the world. He took Matthew—a suave, tricky politician, who knew the political ropes well enough to keep from dangling from one of them by the neck—and, putting the bridle of grace upon him, changed him into an agent of blessing.   [671

POLITICS

... **Church.**   I am not so sure that the corporate body of the church has a right to make political decisions. I am not sure that the leaders of the church have a right to speak, without consultation, for the whole membership of the church. There is no doubt that the American Protestant church came dangerously close in both the 1960 and the 1964 elections to getting involved in politics. Many church bodies openly opposed Kennedy, and four years later many church groups passed resolutions against Goldwater . . . I fear that if the church, as the church, begins to try to dictate in politics, we're way off the main track.   [672

... **Church Leaders.**   I think there are some leaders in the church today—a very small minority, but a very powerful minority—who want political power.   [673

... **God's Purpose.**   In the dome of the Capitol at Washington are inscribed these lines: "One God, one law, one element; And one far-off divine event; To which the whole creation moves." I have often wondered how many congressmen and senators who stand beneath that inscription sense its true interpretation. How perfectly it pictures the feeble efforts of men to rebuild this world according to their own patterns while ignoring God's plans, purposes and program. [674

... Preachers. A President of the United States told me that he was sick and tired of hearing preachers give advice on international affairs when they did not have the facts straight. [675

POOR

... The Church. The church should be deeply concerned about the poor, the illiterate and diseased and those who are oppressed by tyranny and prejudice. [676

POPULARITY

... Christians. When the Christian or the Church becomes popular with the unbelieving world, something is seriously wrong with the Christian or the Church. Because Christ runs counter to evil and because we are Christ-owned, we must also stand against evil. Christians may be shown a grudging respect at times, but if we are faithful to Him, we will surely incur the wrath of the world. [677

PORNOGRAPHY

... Moral Degeneration. Thoughtful people are more and more coming to the inescapable conclusion that the flood of lewd, obscene literature flaunted before our nation's youth—some of it under the thin guise of "art"—is one of the major causes of sex delinquency and crime. [678

POSITIVE ATTITUDE

The Christian religion consists not merely of negations. There is no particular virtue in leaving off all that is bad unless you replace these evil things with positive good, and live life with a positive attitude. [679

POVERTY

... **America And The World.** Did you know that millions in the world today are poverty stricken and we in America are getting richer? The government has great stockpiles of food. I wonder how much longer we can ride in our big cars and our standards of living go higher and higher while the standard of living in India, Asia, and Africa goes down, down, down. Somewhere there is going to be an explosion [680

... **Spiritual.** How many of you are well-to-do? You have a good job, you have an automobile, you have a television set, you have a nice home to go to, you have three square meals a day, you're pretty rich. You have a certain amount of security, but if these are more important than Christ, you have the worst kind of poverty—spiritual poverty. You're very, very, very poor. You have no riches toward God. [681

POWER

The Bible nowhere indicates that God withdraws us from the troubles of life. In fact, we become more involved in life's troubles when we come to Christ. But He gives us power to go on with the battle. [682

PRAYER

Prayer is not our using of God; it more often puts us in a position where God can use us. [683

151

The prayer I ask you to make is this: O God, I am a sinner. I am sorry for my sins. I am willing to turn from them, to change my course. I receive Jesus Christ as my Savior. I confess Him as Lord of my life. From this moment on I want to follow Him in the fellowship of the Church.   [684

... **Answered.** Every religion teaches that men ought to pray, but only the Biblical faith promises that God will answer.   [685

From one end of the Bible to the other there is the record of those whose prayers have been answered—men who turned the tide of history by prayer; men who fervently prayed, and God answered.   [686

... **Attitude.** It is not the body's posture, but the heart's attitude that counts when we pray.   [687

Prayer puts us in the proper attitude to discern the will of God.   [688

... **Children.** Don't force your child to pray. Instead, every night set aside fifteen minutes before his bedtime for reading and conversation. Show him pictures of Jesus, and tell him stories of the Savior. Talk to him of the Heavenly Father. Explain to him that God sends the sun and the rain. Tell him it is God who makes the flowers grow, and gives us food to eat. Then lead him in prayers of thanksgiving and prayers asking the Heavenly Father for guidance and protection.   [689

...Definition Of. Praying is simply a two-way conversation between you and God. [690

...How To Pray. Perhaps you are saying, "But I don't know what to say when I pray." God does not mind your stumbling and faltering phrases. He is not hindered by poor grammar. He is interested in your heart. [691

...Lack Of. About the only time some people get on their knees is when they tune in their television sets. [692

...Need For. If Christianity is to survive in a world filled with materialism, the church must have a revival of prayer. [693

We are living in dangerous times and if there was ever a time that we need to pray, it's now. Because more can be done by prayer than anything else. Prayer is our greatest weapon. [694

...Power Of. In this modern age in which we live, we have learned to harness the power of the mighty Niagara and turn its force to our use and our good. We have learned to hold steam captive in boilers and release its tremendous power to turn our machines and pull our trains. We have learned how to contain gasoline vapors in a cylinder and explode them at the appointed second to move our automobiles and trucks quickly along our highways. We have even discovered the secret of releasing energy in the atom, which is capable of destroying entire cities and civilizations. But very few of us have learned how to fully develop the power of prayer. [695

... **The Right To Pray.** God has a particular responsibility to His children; and unless we have been born into the family of God through the new birth, we have no right to ask favors of God. [696

... **The World.** Today the world is being carried on a rushing torrent of history that is sweeping out of control. There is but one power available to redeem the course of events, and that is the power of prayer by God-fearing, Christ-believing men. [697

... **Why Not Answered.** It may be that your prayers are not answered because of your disobedience to God and lack of faith. [698

PREACHERS

God puts no price tag on the Gift of gifts—it is free! Preachers are not salesmen, for they have nothing to sell. They are the bearers of Good News—the good tidings that Christ died for our sins. [699

PREACHING

... **Emotionalism.** Some people accuse us of too much emotionalism. I say we have too little. That is why we are losing church people to other interests. We need not only to capture their minds, we've got to touch their hearts. We've got to make people feel their faith. [700

PREJUDICE

Prejudice robs its victim of a fair trial in the court of reason. It also kills the opportunity of advancement for those who are its prey. [701

Prejudice, the greatest social evil in the world today, is usually based upon our own ignorance. [702

Prejudice is measured by computing the distance between our own biased opinions and the real truth. If we would all be perfectly honest before God, there would be no prejudice. But since most of us by nature are possessed of biased minds and perverted hearts, prejudice is widespread in the world. [703

PREPARATION

It is strange that we prepare for everything except meeting God. [704

PRIDE

The first, and worst, of the seven deadly sins is pride. It may be spiritual, intellectual, material or social. The most repugnant of these four is spiritual pride. This pride of the spirit was the sin that caused Lucifer, the devil, to fall. This is where sin actually began. [705

...America. There is no sin that God hates more than pride, and America is filled with it. God says, humble yourselves. God demands that we bow in humility at the Cross of Christ and recognize our sinfulness. [706

...Haughtiness. The pride that God loathes is not self-respect or a legitimate sense of personal dignity. It is a haughty, undue self-esteem out of all proportion to our actual worth. Pride may take various forms, but it all emanates from the haughty heart. [707

...Material. In material pride, self is enthroned instead of God. Secondary things are exalted to a place of first importance, and life gets out of balance. [708

...Self Righteousness. Charles Haddon Spurgeon, the great London preacher, was once the guest of a man who made his virtues the chief topic of conversation; but his virtues were all of the negative kind consisting of the bad things he had not done. Disgusted with the man's self-righteousness, Spurgeon said, "Why, man, you are simply a bundle of negatives. You don't drink, you don't gamble, you don't swear. What in the name of goodness do you do?"[709

PROFANITY

The Bible teaches that a man who can control his tongue can control his whole personality. If you cannot control your tongue in the matter of swearing, the Bible teaches that you are in bondage. Profanity is a sin for which God will hold you accountable. [710

PROPHECY

...Bible. The Bible is not only a book of graphic prose, inspirational poetry and dynamic preaching; it is the book of accurate, unerring prophecy. That is to say, it forecasts events before they happen and writes history before it occurs. [711

...Second Advent. God is today raising up among the unbelievers those who are reminding us of the imminence of the second advent of our Lord. [712

...The Last Days. The Bible predicts that in the last days men will have knowledge without wisdom, power without peace, and religion without redemption. [713

PROSPERITY

Currently we are drunk with prosperity. Did ever so many in the history of the world have so much? [714

...Danger Of. Like the Israelites of old, in times of prosperity we have turned to "other gods." We developed our minds and made great material progress, but we neglected the spiritual. [715

PROVIDENCE

...Tragedy. Many times the events that seem tragic in life are allowed by God in order to speak to us. [716

PSYCHIATRY

Psychiatry, a relatively new therapy, can relieve the mind; physicians can help the body; but only God can save the soul. [717

The "anxious seat," or "mourner's bench," of old has been replaced by the psychiatrist's couch. We create our troubles and then try to cure them without God. [718

... **Psychiatrists.** Some time ago it was my privilege to meet with psychiatrists for a luncheon at a famous university. They all agreed that man is so psychologically constituted that he needs to be converted. They also indicated that psychiatry is beginning to realize that it has limitations, and that while it can diagnose cases, it cannot give proper cures. This is where Christ comes in. He is the Great Physician who heals the soul as well as the mind. [719

PSYCHOLOGY

... **Education.** For almost fifty years our educational system has been subject to a kind of psychology which has taught that man is little more than an animal. Our young people have been led to believe that the achievement of happiness is based upon a physical compatibility and that spiritual issues are incidental. It is becoming increasingly obvious that such psychology, having been sown in the wind for fifty years, is now being reaped in the whirlwind of broken homes and tragic lives. [720

... **Morals.** The wave of behavioristic psychology which swept our college campuses and permeated the high school classrooms a few years ago is now ingrained as a way of life for our youth. And we can see the sad results by merely looking around us at the moral decay that is twisting youth to the danger point. [721

... **Sociology.** Psychologists, schooled in the intricate workings of the mind, are confessing that psychology is helpless to solve all of the mental and nervous disturbances of people today. Sociologists, trained in the interactions of society, are admitting that sociology cannot cope with the tremendous problems in human relationships. They all say "there is an answer somewhere else, but we aren't sure where." I can tell them where the answer lies: in the teachings of Jesus Christ—nowhere else! [722

PURPOSE

There's a reason for existence. There's a reason for getting up every morning of the year. I try to tell you that I found that purpose in Jesus Christ, in the scriptures and walking with Him. But you say, "You're crazy, I can't see that." Of course you can't see it. You're blinded! The scales must be removed from your eyes and only Christ can do that. [723

· · R · ·

RACE

Ultimately we are not going to solve the race problem in America until men truly love each other.   [724

...**Bible.** Often I am asked what the Bible has to say about the origin of the races and their various colors of skin. The Bible does not tell us where the skin color comes from, but it does say that we are "made of one blood." It tells us that God, in the sense of creation, is the heavenly Father of all the races.   [725

RACE PROBLEM

...**Psychological.** I suspect that a great part of the race problem in America is psychological rather than biological. There is a psychological barrier that I believe could be overcome by a spiritual renaissance that would plant in our hearts love for each other and the recognition that we are of one blood under heaven.   [726

RACE RELATIONS

...**Integration.** In Chattanooga, Tennessee, back in 1953, we began insisting that our meetings be purposely mixed. I took this stand before the Supreme Court school decision of 1954, and before I had ever heard the word "integration." We just felt it was the Christian thing to do, and that is why the decision was made. [727

... **Problem.** In my ministry I have observed that for true Christians there is no race problem. The ground is level at the cross of Christ. There are no second-class citizens with God. [728

... **Problem; Solution.** There is only one solution to the race problem, and that is a vital, personal experience with Jesus Christ on the part of both races. [729

... **Solution.** It has been my privilege to travel on different continents, and I have observed that in many places where you have two races living side by side there is friction and prejudice. You cannot eliminate this by law alone. Something has to come from the heart. [730

RACIAL SUPERIORITY

The idea of a super race is unBiblical, unScriptural and unChristian. [731

REALITY

... **Escape From.** There are thousands of people who have plans to escape from the realities of life. A new word has come into common usage in the last few years. That word is "escapism." The dictionary defines it as: "A retreat from reality into an imaginary world." But the Bible tells us there is no escape from the realities of life and sin, no escape from the love of God or His judgment. [732

REASON

... **Christianity.** One of the differences I have with some theologians is that they try to reduce the whole content of the Christian faith to an intellectual gymnastic exercise. Christianity cannot be reduced to reason alone. [733

REDEMPTION

The world says that all we need to do is be decent, respectable and reasonable. True, that is all one needs to do to be a member of the Great Society, but to be a member of the Kingdom of God, there must be an inner change. [734

... **Belief.** God calls men to believe in Christ or be lost. Man says that it is enough to be like Christ. Man's goal is imitation, not redemption. [735

... **Definition Of.** The word "redeemed" holds the meaning of a slave who had been enticed into serving one who was not his legal master, but whose real master, intent on recovering the slave's love and service, buys him back at great personal cost. This is what God did for us. [736

... **Mystery.** I cannot comprehend the chemistry and the efficacy of the blood of Christ. There is an element of mystery that cannot be understood with our natural minds. But I do know that all, who by faith, test its power, discover that it can wonderfully change their lives and lift them to a higher plane of living. [737

... **Society.** Fallible men cannot create an infallible society; but redeemed men can redeem society.   [738

REGENERATION

There is only one way to make human nature love instead of hate, and that is through the regeneration that comes as the Spirit of God transforms the heart that comes to the cross asking for forgiveness and cleansing.   [739

RELIGION

... **America.** We talk a great deal of religion in this country, but we need to stop long enough to let our feet catch up with our mouths.   [740

... **Christianity.** We boast that we are a religious nation and so we are, but that doesn't mean that we are Christians.   [741

... **Churches.** Many church members are exposed to just enough religion to let their souls go to hell.   [742

... **Counterfeit.** The inescapable implication of a counterfeit is that the real thing exists. No one ever counterfeited a seventy-five-dollar bill. Every counterfeit bears witness to the reality of the currency it copies. So in the midst of all the plans and programs men have devised to satisfy their religious urge, true religion does exist and is available for all who will come to God on His terms.   [743

... **Faith.** You can't come to Christ intellectually. So many people make the mistake. They try to figure it all out.

You can't do it. You have to come by faith. And you have to come as a simple little child would come. And when you do He comes in your heart, He forgives your sins, He adopts you into His family and you become a child of God. [744

... **God.** Christian joy is dependent on a personal relationship with God, and not on externals. [745

... **Gospel.** I wouldn't walk across the street to interest anyone in religion; but I'd be willing to go anywhere in the world to preach the Gospel of the Son of God. [746

Religion is the story of what a sinful man tries to do for a holy God. The Gospel is the wonderful story of what a holy God has done for sinful man. There are thousands of religions, but only one gospel. [747

... **Intellect.** True religion, contrary to the conception of some, increases your intellect rather than detracts from it. [748

... **Joy Of.** It has been thought by many that to be religious is to be serious and even gloomy. Jesus did not teach it this way. He said: "Peace I leave with you, My peace I give unto you." The Psalmist said: "In Thy presence is fullness of joy," and Paul said: "Rejoice in the Lord and again I say Rejoice." These are not the sayings of advocates of a gloomy and desolate religion. Christianity gives men and women a song and a smile, no matter what the circumstances are. [749

...**Lack Of.** Many people have been inoculated with a little religion, so they have just enough to keep them from finding the real Jesus Christ. [750

...**Mistake.** We have made the mistake of dividing our lives into neat little compartments—politics in one section, economics in another, and religion poked back in a dark, little corner—brought out for display only for a few minutes on Sunday morning. [751

...**Pretense.** A religion which is full of pretense is nothing but religious addiction. [752

...**Psychology.** For years psychiatrists had little time for Biblical faith, but now experts urge religion and psychology to join hands to help the multitudes of mentally ill persons in the world. [753

...**Teachers.** There are some teachers of religion who try deliberately to destroy the authority of the Scriptures and the faith of the church. [754

...**Universities.** In many universities, religion is frowned on, and Brigitte Bardot is idolized. [755

...**World Brotherhood.** There is no common denominator in the world today except religion. The world has become a neighborhood without brotherhood. [756

...**World's Definition.** We must not accept the world's definitions of what it means to be religious. We must accept the definitions given us in the Bible. They alone are valid. [757

RELIGIOUS CONVICTIONS

Not only in the social and political arenas of American life are we afraid. In our religious convictions, we're afraid to speak out. [758

RELIGIOUS EDUCATION

...**Christian Experience.** Much of the philosophy of religious education has been based upon a false premise, and perhaps many have missed the essence of Christian experience, having had religious training take its place. [759

RELIGIOUS WARS

I think the Crusades were inconsistent with the teachings of the Gospel. So many of the religious wars of history, which were fought in the name of Christianity, were waged by people who never really knew Christ or the love of Christ. [760

REPENTANCE

...**America.** God is looking for real and genuine repentance. To whom much is given, much is required. Much is given to America. I tell you much shall be required of America. God cannot send a revival until we pay the price. God cannot send a revival until Christians are willing to pay the price. [761

...**Definition.** Repentance is the launching pad where the soul is sent on its eternal orbit with God at the center of the arc. [762

...Faith. This is a time for repentance and faith. It is a time for soul-searching to see if our anchor holds.[763

...Prodigal Son. The prodigal son imagined that the pleasures of the far-off city were greater than the joys of his home. But after wasting his substance in riotous living, he returned to his father in repentance and tears, and begged to be a hired servant in his father's house. His tuition in the school of experience was very costly, but he discovered that real peace was found in facing up to the reality of life and doing something about it. [764

...Results Of. Christ can give you power to overcome every sin and habit in your life. He can break the ropes, fetters and chains of sin; but you must repent, confess, commit and surrender yourself to Him first. [765

RESPECT
...For God. Respect for God always engenders a respect for the dignity of the individual; and when God finds no place in our lives and in our talk, disrespect for others flows out of the cesspool of our conversation. [766

RESPONSIBILITY
...Rebellion. Throughout the behavior of parents, teachers, and teen-agers alike there seems to run the theme of freedom from responsibility, which leads directly to rebellion. [767

RESURRECTION
The death of Jesus on the Cross removed the last barrier between God and man. With the words, "It is finished,"

He announced that the road from man to God was completed and open to traffic.   [768

... **Bodily.** The Bible teaches the bodily resurrection of Christ. It is not simply a spiritual resuscitation, as some would have us believe. His very body was raised by God from the dead, and some day we shall see the nailprints in His hands.   [769

... **Christianity.** The Christian faith alone points to an empty tomb and claims that its Founder rose from the dead.   [770

... **Evidence Of.** There is more evidence that Jesus rose from the dead than there is that Julius Caesar ever lived or that Alexander the Great died at the age of thirty-three.[771

... **Historical Proof.** I don't believe there's a fact in ancient history that is so well proven as the resurrection of Jesus Christ. But, even if there were no historical proof, no scientific proof, I would still believe it, because I believe the Bible is God's inspired Word. The Bible reveals how the whole early church went up and down the country preaching the resurrection of Jesus Christ. This was what shook the Roman Empire—that a man had risen from the dead, that He was alive, that death could not hold Him.   [772

... **Salvation.** Without a belief in the resurrection, there can be no personal salvation.   [773

... **Truth.** The resurrection of Christ is the chief proof of the Christian faith. It is the truth which lies at the very foundation of the Gospel. Other doctrines may be important, but the resurrection is essential. [774

REVIVAL

... **Churches.** The revival we long for must begin in our churches. Our churches are going to have to repent of their sins, their worldliness, strife, pride, bickering, malice, backbiting, and intolerance of each other—Pharisees on the one side and Sadducees on the other. [775

... **Requirements For.** Four things we must do: we must humble ourselves; secondly, we must pray; thirdly, we must seek His face; and fourthly, we must forsake our sins. Then, the Bible says, we are ready for the great and mighty revival that God will send. [776

... **World-Wide.** Crisis times are times when Christ should be proclaimed. Although there has never been a world-wide revival, I believe we may be on the verge of one now. [777

REVOLUTIONARIES

... **Moral.** Our way lies not in human ingenuity, but in a return to God. The early Church had moral revolutionaries; we need moral revolutionaries today. America doesn't need more nuclear weapons or more armies. America needs men and women to live for Christ. [778

RICH

... **Americans.** You are a rich man, a rich woman, a rich

boy, a rich girl, in comparison with the population of the world, if you have shoes on, if you have a suit of clothes on, if you have a dress on. You're rich if you've had a meal today. [779

... **Poor.** We are rich in the things that perish, but poor in the things of the spirit. We are rich in gadgets, but poor in faith. We are rich in goods, but poor in grace. We are rich in know-how, but poor in character. We are rich in words, but poor in deeds. [780

RIGHTEOUSNESS
... **Gift of God.** Righteousness is something which we do not possess as a natural gift, but it is a God-given gift to be specially received. [781

ROMANCE
The word "romance," according to the dictionary, means excitement, adventure and something extremely real. Romance should last a lifetime. Some people say that when the honeymoon is over and they face the hard realities of married life, it isn't the same any more. They expect the romance to fade when the honeymoon is over, and it surely will fade if two people try to go it alone. Only if Christ is a partner in the home and in the hearts of the two people will romance continue. [782

ROME
... **America.** The same symptoms that were in Rome in its last days are seen and felt in America today. [783

RULES FOR CHRISTIAN LIFE

The Christian life carries with it grave responsibilities which cannot be met without following certain rules.

First: You should read your Bible daily.

Second: Learn the secret of prayer.

Third: Rely constantly on the Holy Spirit.

Fourth: Attend church regularly.

Fifth: Be a witnessing Christian.

Sixth: Let love be the ruling principle of your life.

Seventh: Be an obedient Christian.

Eighth: Learn how to meet temptation.

Ninth: Be a wholesome Christian.

Tenth: Live above your circumstances. [784

RUSSIA

...Moralistic. Russia is a moralistic country because they have found, by trial and error, that you can't build a strong society unless you have certain moral laws. But their concept of morality is very different from ours. For example, lying is all right if it achieves their ends; sexual immorality, too. Killing can be a virtuous thing, if it's done for the ultimate cause of the state. They do have a kind of morality, but it is contrary to Christian morality. [785

· · S · ·

SACRAMENT

A true sacrament is not a mere creed, or ordinance, or form, but it is a life of service to God and to man. The most eloquent prayer is the prayer through hands that heal and bless. The highest form of worship is the worship of unselfish Christian service. The greatest form of praise is the sound of consecrated feet seeking out the lost and helpless.   [786

SALVATION

Knowing about Christ, the cross, and the way of salvation is one thing, and appropriating it to yourself is quite another.   [787

Personal salvation is not an occasional rendezvous with Deity; it is an actual dwelling with God. Christianity is not just an avocation; it is a lifelong, eternity-long vocation. [788

. . . Cost Of.   General Eisenhower, the day before D Day, said to his troops, "There is no victory at bargain prices." There is not going to be a short cut to victory in any war. Men have to go out and fight and die. And, as in war, there is no short cut to the victory of God. It took the blood of Christ and it'll take you denying self and taking up a cross and following Him to gain salvation. [789

...Discipline. Salvation is indeed a gift of God, but there is a sense in which we "work out (our) own salvation with fear and trembling." His creative action takes place through our obedient action, and He is able to work when we work. We receive the new life as a free gift, but we must practice that life if we are to live victoriously in a period of crisis. And it is impossible to live a victorious life without careful discipline. [790

...God. The world today offers many saviors, but none of them saves to the uttermost. The world today offers many panaceas, but they cannot reach to the depths of our depravity. The world today offers many shortcuts to salvation; but to be truly saved, we must be reconciled to God.[791

...Meaning Of. Salvation is not just repairing the original self. It is a new self created of God in righteousness and true holiness. [792

...New Birth, Personal. The night I came to Jesus Christ in Charlotte in 1934, I really wasn't any different the next morning. I looked the same. I dressed the same. I carried the same lunch box to school. I played on the same team, had the same friends. But you know when I got up that morning I knew the world was different. I hadn't had any emotion the night before when I had accepted Christ. To me it was a very non-emotional thing. I just walked up in simple faith, not really understanding anything about it. If you had asked me the next day what had happened to me, I couldn't have told you. I didn't know. And I'm sure if anybody had come with a survey they'd say, "Well, just strike him out; he didn't know what he was doing last night." But down deep inside of me I knew something was different. I couldn't tell you what it was. But from then on my life took on a new dimension. I started in a new direction. Now I stumbled around. I didn't have anybody to tell me to start reading the Bible and praying. You know, I went back to church and I had always thought we had the dreariest, most boring preacher on earth. He was one of the sweetest, godliest saints I ever knew and I remember him with warm affection, but I thought he was the worst preacher that had ever lived. But after I had accepted Christ the next Sunday morning, I said, "Mother, you know Dr. Lindsay certainly preached a great sermon this morning." She said, "Well, son, it wasn't Dr. Lindsay's preaching; he preached the same. You're different. You now know Christ." [793

... **The Cross.** The Bible teaches that the cross is God's testimony to the fact that there is no other way of salvation. [794

SANCTIFICATION

When Christ comes into the human heart, a process begins that the Bible calls sanctification. You begin to grow in the Grace and Knowledge of Christ toward spiritual maturity. [795

174

Sanctification actually means "separated" or "clean." In one sense, sanctification is instantaneous. The moment you receive Christ as Savior, the Holy Spirit comes into your heart. There is also a sense in which sanctification is progressive. You grow in the grace and knowledge of Jesus Christ. [796

SATAN

...**Defeat Of.** Whenever I am conscious of satan's presence, I try to follow the formula once offered by a little girl: "When satan knocks, I just send Christ to the door." [797

...**Immorality.** Satan fails to speak of the remorse, the futility, the loneliness and the spiritual devastation which goes hand in hand with immorality. [798

...**Man.** With every year that passes, the link between satan's mind and the minds of millions of human beings becomes stronger. This arch demon is pumping a swelling stream of filth into the world. All of this is the inevitable result of man's rebellion against God and his fall into sin. [799

...**Negation.** Nothing could please satan more than for Christians to fall into the rut of negation. [800

...**Power Of.** I believe that the Bible teaches that there is a personality called "Satan," and that he is the author of evil. Where he came from is a mystery. But he's a mighty power, and he's in conflict with the forces of God. Now when satan comes, he doesn't come with a sign here and

175

say, "I'm Satan—watch out!" The Bible says he comes as an angel of light. He counterfeits. He comes close to the real thing. And you see today, I think, satan producing counterfeits in religion, and you have false teachers who are leading many people away.   [801

SAVIOR

God says that Christ is the Savior of the world. Man says that Christ is just a great example.   [802

SCHOOLS

... **God.** A generation or more ago we took God out of our educational systems and thought we could get away with it. We have laughed at God, religion and the Bible. Now the Supreme Court has ordered the Bible out of our schools. We are sowing the wind and we are surely going to reap the whirlwind.   [803

... **Religion.** I violently disagree with those who throw God and religion out of our schools.   [804

SCIENCE

I don't think there is any conflict at all between science and the Scriptures. I think we have misinterpreted the Scriptures many times, and we have tried to make the Scriptures say things that they weren't meant to say. The Bible is not a book of science. The Bible is a book of redemption.   [805

... **Bible.** If you are told that science has disproved the Bible, ask specifically where such is the case. True science and a true understanding of the Bible are never at variance. [806

...**Faith.** There comes a step beyond which I cannot go intellectually. I must say that by faith I believe. Because almost every proposition, whether in science or anywhere else, is taken by faith. [807

SCRIPTURES

...**Church.** One of the greatest needs in the American Church today is a revival of faith in the Scriptures. [808

SECOND COMING OF CHRIST

The most often mentioned event in the entire Bible is the second coming of Christ. The new birth is mentioned nine times, baptism twenty times, repentance seventy times, but the second coming of Christ is mentioned more than 300 times in the New Testament. [809

...**End Of The World.** The Bible teaches that the end will come with the coming again of Jesus Christ, and that He will set up a kingdom of righteousness and social justice where hatred, greed and jealousy will no longer be known. [810

...**Reaction.** I am convinced that if Christ came back today, He would be crucified more quickly than He was 2,000 years ago. [811

...**Reasons.** Jesus will come to the earth a second time. He came the first time as the Man of sorrows; He will come

the second time as the mighty God. He came the first time as
the Lamb of God; He will come the second time as the Lion
of the tribe of Judah. He came the first time as the Prince of
Peace; He will come the second time as King of kings and
Lord of lords. He came the first time as the Author of
salvation; He will come the second time as the Finisher of
our faith. He came the first time to atone for sin; He will
come the second time to judge sinners. [812

SECURITY

Modern psychiatrists say that one of the basic needs of
man is security. In God we have the greatest of security.[813

... **Collegiate Conformity.** On campus the quickest
way to security is through the crowd. Precisely where students talk about being independent and on their own, you
will find them practicing the most rigid conformity in dress,
in speech, in moral attitudes and in thinking. Sometimes
they follow fashion at the expense of integrity. [814

... **Love.** Nothing can bring a real sense of security into
the home except true love. [815

SELF-CENTEREDNESS

Self-centeredness is the basic cause of much of our distress
in life. Hypochondria, a mental disorder which is accompanied by melancholy and depression, is often caused by self-
pity and self-centeredness. [816

SELF-CONTROL

... **Speech.** You have a tongue and a voice. These instruments of speech can be used destructively or employed constructively. You can use your tongue to slander, to gripe, to scold, to nag, and to quarrel; or you can bring it under the control of God's Spirit and make it an instrument of blessing and praise.   [817

SELF-DENIAL

The Bible says that to be a true follower of Jesus Christ you must deny yourself. You must deny your self-life—the flesh, the natural man. The self-life manifests itself in self-indulgence, self-love, self-will, self-seeking, self-pride. [818

... **Meaning Of.**   The denial of self means to renounce self and accept Christ as Master, to cease living a self-centered life; to surrender self completely to Him.   [819

SELF-DISCIPLINE

Christians today bear little resemblance to those of the first century. We twentieth-century Christians have become soft. We have become absorbed with the world, until it is now difficult to tell the difference between the Christian and the worldling. The Bible teaches that every Christian is to live a life of self-discipline. We Christians need to tighten our belts and harden ourselves for the trials that lie ahead.   [820

SELFISHNESS

... **Christianity-Communism.**   Communism, with its multiplied millions of adherents, promises to help the helpless. Unless Christians break with their selfishness and begin to help these millions of starving people out of their misery, they will turn to the only other alternative—communism. [821

. . . Love. True love is never selfish, and love will die if it is not fed by thoughtfulness, courtesy, kindness and work. [822

. . . Poverty-Privilege. Three-fifths of the world live in squalor, misery and hunger. Too long have the privileged few exploited and ignored the underprivileged millions of the world. Our selfishness is at long last catching up with us. Unless we begin to act, to share and to do something about this great army of starving humanity, God will judge us. [823

. . . Sin. Because selfishness is at the root of most of our sin, Jesus said: "He that would save his life will lose it, and he that loses his life will save it." [824

Selfishness is one of the greatest sins, if not the greatest sin in the world today. Selfishness: myself above everybody else. You trample anybody. You push anybody aside. You might do it with a smile, but you are working to push self forward all the time. That is sin. [825

SELF-LOVE

You have an ego—a consciousness of being an individual! Of course you do. But that doesn't mean that you are to worship yourself, to think constantly of yourself, and to live entirely for self. [826

180

SELF-PITY

... **Compassion.** Tears shed for self are tears of weakness, but tears shed for others are a sign of strength.   [827

SELF-RESPECT

... **Self-Deception.** Self-respect is a wonderful thing so long as it is not produced by self-deception.   [828

SELF-SACRIFICE

The self-sacrifice of God's gentry through the centuries has contributed immeasurably to our culture, to our ethics and to our faith. Down deep we know that there are still things worth dying for, that an existence void of faith is still a fate worse than death.   [829

SELF-SUFFICIENCY

It seems to be man's nature to want to be self-sufficient, to work out a righteousness of his own, to climb up to heaven some other way than by the manner which God proposes.   [830

SELF-UNDERSTANDING

How many of us are leading a double life? We are two people. In church on a Sunday morning you are one person —in school you are a person—but when you are alone or out with the gang or in your automobile, you are another person. But you see, that's where God has the advantage—because God sees you in the dark, too.   [831

SEX

Sex is a gift from God—not only for the propagation of the race, but for enjoyment—but only in the bonds of matrimony. Sex is a creative energy and can be a tremendous dynamo for good in life, if directed in the right direction. [832

... **America; Obsession.** America has a greater obsession with sex than Rome ever had. [833

... **Bible.** The Bible does not say sex is sin. This sex urge which comes to girls at 13 or 14 years of age, and a little later for the boys, is not a sin. Don't let anybody tell you it's dirty, either. It's not. It's a gift from God. The Bible has a lot to say about it. And we ought to teach children what the Bible says about it. God gave it to people for two reasons, to propagate the race and to provide climax and fulfillment of true love within the bonds of matrimony . . . but only in the bonds of matrimony. [834

... **Degeneracy Of.** Man with his vile, self-destructive, sinful, rebellious nature has taken what was intended to be the most glorious and complete act of love between two people and has made it something low, cheap and filthy. Sex relations, stripped of mutual love and respect and a sincere desire to give joy and fulfillment within the holy bonds of matrimony, degenerate into the lowest forms of immorality and animalism. [835

... **Obsession.** When people lose their way, their purpose, their will and their goals, as well as their faith, like the ancient Israelites they go "a whoring." [836

... **Satan's Deception.** Satan can transform himself

into an angel of light and deceive even Christians. Thus impurity has a better press agent than purity. Satan, in selling sex wholesale, plays up the momentary thrill; but the consequences of this vicious sin are played down.   [837

... **Self-Control.**   There must be firm control of the sex impulses. This God-given instinct has been dragged through the gutter by modern thinking, and we have made a cheap toy out of the most sacred gifts God has ever given to man. Our procreative powers need to be dedicated to Christ. [838

... **Stimulation.**   Sex stimulation comes at us from every direction now, and there is no way to guarantee you living a clean, pure life—except by the help of Christ. The mark of a Christian is self-control and self-discipline.   [839

... **Students.**   Much of the sexual conduct of students can be traced to insecurity, an absence of proper home training, the emptiness of the money-and-prestige-oriented, merry-go-round life of today, and the absence of a genuine experience with Christ.   [840

... **Worship.**   To read the papers and magazines you would think that we were almost worshipping the female bosom. It has always been the mark of decaying civilizations to become obsessed with sex. . . . Many do something for a thrill, only to find the next time that they must increase the dose to produce the same thrill. As the kick wears off, they are driven to look for new means, for different experiences to produce comparable kick. The sex glutton is tormented by feelings of guilt and remorse. His mode of living is saturated with intense strain, unnatural emotions and inner conflicts. [841

SHARING

God has given us hands and hearts, for receiving and sharing. [842

SILENCE

... **Guilt.** Our silence makes us guilty, for "silence gives consent." At the martyrdom of Stephen, Saul of Tarsus cast no stones. Yet in standing mutely by, he was consenting to Stephen's death. [843

... **Involvement.** The motto of many people seems to be, "Stay aloof. Don't get involved. Let somebody else speak out." [844

... **When It Is Wrong.** In the face of the mounting crime wave threatening every family in the free world, too many of us find ourselves afflicted with moral laryngitis.[845

SIN

... **A Threat.** Sin is a grim fact. It stands like a titanic force,—a threat—contesting all the good that men may try to accomplish. It stands like a dark shadow, ever ready to blot out whatever light may reach us from on high. [846

... **Bible.** The Bible tells us that sin is more than overt acts that cause difficulties and troubles in this life. The Bible teaches that sin is an offense to God.   [847

   ... **Brings Death.**   The Bible says, when sin is finished, it brings forth death.   [848

   ... **Consequences.**   Divorce, alcoholism and immorality are direct results of the restlessness of sin.   [849

   ... **Consequences Of.**   The three chief consequences of sin are: estrangement from God; bondage to self; disharmony with others.   [850

   ... **Crime.**   In discussing the present crime crisis in the United States, a well-known news magazine summed it up by saying, "There's a mystery about this phenomenon that we cannot understand." The Bible teaches that this is the mystery of iniquity; and the mystery of iniquity is the power unseen, except by its effects, which is ever working in the world for evil: Sin!   [851

   ... **Death.**   The Bible always links sin and death. You seldom find one mentioned without the other.   [852

   ... **Definition.**   Sin is anything contrary to the will and law of God.   [852-A

There are many words in the New Testament that are translated "sin." One of the commonest is hamartia. It means "a missing of the target." Sin is the missing of the target at which life must aim and which life ought to hit.[853

... Destruction. If you have been trying to escape sin in amusement and sinful pleasure, I beg of you to turn back. This is a blind alley that leads to destruction and death. You cannot find eternal joy, happiness, peace and pleasure on that road. [854

... Ease Of. The Scripture teaches that the more sins we commit, the easier it becomes to sin. [855

... Moral Disease. We've told the people of our society that they're psychologically sick, but we've neglected to tell them that they're sinners in the sight of God, that they have a moral disease, that this disease is called sin, and that they need salvation, conversion and redemption. [856

... None Is New. There are no new sins—only new sinners; there are no new crimes—only new criminals; no new evils—only new evil-doers; no new pleasures—only new pleasure-seekers. [857

... Omission. The sin of doing nothing has been called the sin of omission—which is just as dangerous as the sin of commission. [858

... Origin Of. Sin entered the human race through Adam, and the human race has been trying without success to get rid of it ever since. [859

... Pay. Sin pays—but it pays off in remorse, regret and failure. [860

...**Pleasure, Consequences.**   The Bible says there is a pleasure in sin. You can go out and get drunk and have a good time for a few hours. You can go out in the back seat of an automobile at a drive-in theater with your girl and commit immorality for a few minutes. That's the pleasure of sin. But—oh the consequences—the guilt—the tormenting conscience! Most of all, you will face the judgment of an angry God. Is it worth it? We buy most everything on the installment plan today and you can't sin for cash, you can only sin on the installment plan. You sin today, you spend the rest of your life paying for it, and then eternity. Is it worth it? [861

...**Responsibility.**   But God does not excuse sin. He holds us morally responsible. He considers it so terrible and so important that He sent His Son to the cross to die for it.   [862

There are many today who ascribe sin to psychological causes. Many say that they are not responsible for what they do. But God says that we are responsible.   [863

...**Separation From God.**   Sin is the only thing that can separate us from God or induce Him to hide His face from us. It dishonors Him. With it, we can have no fellowship. No matter how small the sin is, it can shut out our prayers from the ears of God.   [864

...**Sinful Thinking.**   The Bible teaches that all sin begins with sinful thinking.   [865

...**Sinner.**   Any man that says he is not a sinner, the Bible says is a liar.   [866

...Thought. Evil thoughts and imagination, if nourished and fed, will eventually lead to actual sin.   [867

...Vicarious. People read these cheap novels and get a vicarious, imaginative thrill out of the experiences they read. There are people that go to movies, or watch television dramas, or listen to soap operas, and then dream that they, themselves, are living the same type of lives. The Bible calls this "sin."   [868

SINCERITY

Sincerity is the hallmark of the Christian faith. It was born in the white heat of spiritual conflict, and it will never be maintained by half-hearted, half-committed, halfway disciples.   [869

...Redemption. The fact remains that there are no curative powers in sincerity, and there is no healing balm in an ethical idealism apart from redemption.   [870

SIXTH SENSE

Man has five physical senses: he can see, hear, taste, smell and touch. He is more than a body; he is a living soul. His soul is that part of his being which possesses intelligence, conscience and memory—the real personality. That soul has a "sixth sense"—the ability to believe, to have faith.   [871

SLOTHFULNESS

The sin of slothfulness extends into many areas, such as: being slothful about your driving habits on the highway that endanger the lives of others; being slothful about your per-

sonal cleanliness, which is next to Godliness; being slothful about the smile that should be upon the face of every
Christian at all times, no matter what the circumstances;
being slothful about helping those that are in need in your
neighborhood; being slothful about giving to charity, in
order that the unfortunate and the underprivileged may
have the necessities of life.   [872

SMOKING

There is good reason why Christians speak out against the
use of tobacco. The Bible teaches that when a man is converted to Christ and receives pardon for his sin, Christ enters
into his heart to dwell. Having come to dwell, we are then to
regard the human body as sacred. "Your body is a temple of
the Holy Spirit which is in you, which you have from God,
and ye are not your own. For ye were bought with a price;
glorify God therefore in your body." And smoking is, quite
obviously, detrimental to the temple of the body.   [873

SOCIAL APPLICATION

. . . Gospel.   If the gospel we preach does not have a
social application, if it will not work effectively in the work-
a-day world, then it is not the gospel of Jesus Christ.   [874

SOCIAL ISSUES

Even a casual study of the life of Jesus reveals that He
was interested in man's response to the social problems he
faces.   [875

I believe in taking a stand on moral, social, and spiritual
issues. I had not been preaching long before I decided that I

would never preach to another segregated audience. I felt this was the Christian position. In our crusades, I have preached on every conceivable social issue. Our radio program has touched on every social issue of our day. [876

SOCIAL PROBLEMS

... Answer To. Christ has an answer to the social problems. He can meet them in triumph. In this field He has a far greater program than Marx, Engels or Lenin. But we have failed to capitalize on this fact. [877

... Broken Homes. The broken home has become the Number One social problem of America, and could ultimately lead to the destruction of our civilization. [878

SOCIAL REFORM

... Jesus. Jesus was one of the greatest social reformers, but He accomplished it by transforming the individual. He was not a revolutionist, He was the Redeemer; but by redeeming the individual personality, He brought about many social reforms. [879

SOCIETY

A society has been defined as "a group living together under the same environment and regarded as constituting a homogeneous unit or entity." Though our American society possibly more nearly approximates this definition than any group of people in the world, we in America are still racked at this hour with painful divisions, deep hatreds, gross misunderstandings and great social injustices. Though the Great Society may be a noble objective, we have a great distance to go before we even come close to living up to that name. [880

...**Great.** The "great society" concept is not new. Plato formulated his "Republic"; Sir Thomas More his "Utopia"; Karl Marx his "classless society"; and many others have made attempts to create a picture of the ideal social order. But while the motivation may have been genuinely humanitarian, past efforts have failed miserably. The dreams have cracked up on the rocks of reality.   [881

...**Kingdom.** How does the Kingdom Society differ from the other societies that men are devising today? First, conversion is a requirement of citizenship. The kingdoms of this world do not require a change in human nature. Second, the Kingdom Society is built upon love rather than hate. The way of the world is hate and tyranny and chaos. Third, the Kingdom Society is not built on the profit motive. The verb of the world is "get." The verb of the Christian is "give." Fourth, the form of government in the Kingdom Society is unique. It is not a democracy in which the people govern, but a "Christocracy" in which Christ is the supreme authority. And finally, the Kingdom Society is lasting. The history of man has been an unending succession of half-successes and total failures. Twenty-six civilizations have come and gone, and man still battles the same problems, over and over and over again. He solves one issue only to be confronted by one three times more difficult.   [882

SORROW

...**Choices.** When Harry Lauder, the great Scottish comedian, received word that his son had been killed in France, he said: "In a time like this, there are three courses open to man: He may give way to despair and become bitter. He may endeavor to drown his sorrow in drink or in a life of wickedness. Or he may turn to God." In your sorrow, I beg of you—turn to God. [883

SOUL

. . . Bodily Appetites. In the world in which we live, we give too much attention to satisfying the appetites of the body and practically none to the soul. Consequently we are one-sided. We become fat physically and materially, while spiritually we are lean, weak, and anemic. [884

SPEAKING

Jesus talked with such simplicity that the common people heard Him gladly. [885

. . . Think First. We should ask ourselves three questions before we speak: Is it true? Is it kind? Does it glorify Christ? If we would always think before we speak, there would be much less evil speaking and there would soon be a spiritual awakening and a revival that would sweep the church in America. [886

SPIRIT

. . . Fruit Of. The Bible also teaches us that the Spirit of God produces the fruit of the Spirit. The fruit of the Spirit is love, joy, peace, long-suffering, gentleness, goodness, faith, meekness and temperance. Now these things, these nine things, nine clusters of fruit, are to characterize the life of every Christ-born child of God. [887

. . . Sins Of. There are many Christians who would not dare do certain worldly things, and yet they are filled with pride, gossiping, malice and sins of the spirit that are far more worldly and evil in God's sight than some of these outward things. [888

SPIRITUAL AWAKENING

The great need in America is not a new organization. The great need in America is not more economic prosperity. The great need in America is a great spiritual awakening; a revival in which men and women will humble themselves and pray and turn from their wicked ways to the God of our fathers. We, as Americans, whether we realize it or not, are living in a fish-bowl and the whole world is looking in to see how we live. My travels throughout the world lead me to believe that America has the greatest responsibility and obligation and opportunity that any nation has ever had in the world. [889

SPIRITUAL DISEASE

When we have a physical need, we go to the doctor. When we recognize that we have a moral and spiritual disease, we must go to the Great Physician, our Lord and Savior Jesus Christ. [890

SPIRITUAL ILLUMINATION

Christ indicated that only those who have spiritual illumination and discernment from the Holy Spirit can understand the trends and meaning of history. [891

SPIRITUAL LIFE

The great transition is not in death. The great transition is from spiritual death to spiritual life. When you receive

Christ, that's the big change. Has that happened to you? [892

There are many people who say that their spiritual life is living the Sermon on the Mount, but the man or woman is yet to be born who has ever lived up to the Sermon on the Mount. [893

SPIRITUAL NECESSITY

Any philosophy which deals only with the here and now is not adequate for man, whom God created a living soul, in His own image and likeness. Unless we can cope with our spiritual problems, we are left empty, frustrated, and defeated. [894

SPIRITUAL STRENGTH

...America. Almost none of the leaders of the free world believe we will be defeated militarily, but many fear we lack the spiritual strength to endure for another generation. [895

SPIRITUAL VISION

You may have 20-20 vision but spiritually you're blind because the Bible says you have two sets of eyes. You have eyes in the soul, and the Bible teaches that those eyes have been blinded by satan. One of the difficulties with our world leaders today is that they don't know spiritual things. They don't know the cause of the world problems and they don't know the cure. Sometimes the UN reminds me of a blind man. They're trying to put this war out and this trouble spot out and they're doing their best—but they don't understand the disease. They lack spiritual vision. [896

STEPMOTHERS

It is unfortunate that the word "stepmother" has too often fallen into disrepute. Some of the most noble women I know are stepmothers. To become a stepmother is much more difficult than being a mother. [897

STEWARDSHIP

If God has given you more than your neighbors round about you, dedicate it to Christ, and realize that you are only a steward of that which God has given you—and some day you will have to give an account for every penny you spent. [898

SUFFERING

Christians are called to suffer. God does not promise Christians an easy pathway to heaven, nor does He promise flowery beds of ease. [899

"What do you know about the suffering of Christ?" someone asked me. "You have never suffered." I answered: When a Western Union messenger delivers a death message to a home, he doesn't take part in all the suffering connected with the message. He just delivers the telegram. That's all I am—God's messenger boy. I don't ask people to look up to Billy Graham. I ask them to respect Jesus Christ. I didn't die on a cross. Neither did you. But Christ did. He suffered and died for our sins. [900

. . . Reasons For. "Why does God allow fear to continue to grip the hearts of men in this enlightened age? Where is God's power? Why doesn't He stop all this misery and cruelty with which our age has been cursed? If God is good and merciful, why are men and women crushed by agonies almost beyond their endurance?" Questions like these are asked not only by atheists and enemies of religion, but also by bewildered Christians, who, staggering under the burden of anguish, cry out, "Why must I bear this misery? How can God lay all this suffering on me?" The word of God teaches that Christians suffer in order that they might glorify God in their lives. [901

SUICIDE

If you have given yourself completely to Christ and are absolutely surrendered to His control, there can be no thought of suicide. [902

SUNDAY SCHOOL

I am convinced that the Sunday School is the greatest single agency for teaching people God's Word, as well as a tremendous evangelistic force in its own right. [903

SUPERFICIALITY

This century could well go down in history, not so much as a century of progress, but as "the century of superficiality." [904

SURRENDER

If you are a Christian and have been suffering defeat, and have been outside the will of God, and do not know the power and thrill and joy that Christ can bring, I beg of you to surrender every area of your life. Give yourself wholly to Christ. [905

·· T ··

TEACHERS

... Sunday School. Every Sunday School teacher is just as much called of God as a missionary to the heart of Africa. He needs to prepare just as diligently—he needs to labor just as earnestly—as if he were carrying the Gospel to the most remote spot on the globe. [906

TEENAGERS

... Adults. No longer do teenagers act like adults. Adults act like teenagers. Every time the teenagers get something good going, the adults adopt it. We are told to act young, think young. And industries spend millions of dollars every year to find out what the teenagers really want. [907

... Blame. Do not blame the teenagers entirely for any problems they have; their difficulties stem from the environment we have created for them. [908

... Problems. The juvenile problem has become so alarming that some people wonder if there is any hope. Teenage gang warfare makes Al Capone of a generation ago look like a sissy. [909

... Rebellion. Today we find teenagers rioting, demonstrating, rebelling. Newspapers are filled with stories and statistics of youth crime. In many of our major cities the teenage gangs are teeming disorganized armies with their peculiar dress, their language, and their homemade weapons. When I speak to young people, I see their faces and see the youthful longing, the questing, the wishful dreaming and hoping. And I ask myself, who has failed these young people? Certainly the home must bear a major responsibility. Parents have failed to spend time with their children, they have failed to love their children.   [910

... Two Kinds. There are two kinds of teenagers. As I travel around the country I find that the vast majority of young people are young people with courage and purpose and reason. They are the people who are pouring into the Peace Corps and the missionary service, into churches, into military service. They are out helping others. They have wholesome ideals, and thousands upon thousands of them are religious young people. But on the other side of the coin I find another kind of young person—rebellious, bored, no purpose, no reason for existence—he doesn't know where he came from, why he's here, or where he's going. These are the young people that make the headlines that we read in our papers. They are the ones that have become delinquent.   [911

TEMPTATION

... Christian. There is nothing unusual or abnormal about a Christian being tempted. Indeed, he should expect it.   [912

...**Meaning.** Temptation of the devil does not mean that your life is not right with God. It is actually a sign that you are right with God.   [913

...**Not A Sin.** Every one of us is tempted. There is no sin in being tempted. Jesus was tempted. The sin is when you use the temptation as an excuse for giving in to it. [914

...**Reaction To.** Everyone meets temptations, but some folks entertain them.   [915

...**Satan.** God never tempts any man. That is satan's business; he is the tempter, and he tempts us along the lines of our natural desires.   [916

THEOLOGY
...**Theologians.** The pressure today on a theologian in a seminary is just like it is on a professor in a university: It's to get something new. It's to get a new approach, a new angle, and therefore to become a prominent, quoted theologian whose books are read.   [917

THOUGHTS
...**Acts.** If your thoughts are evil, then your acts will be evil. If your thoughts are godly, then your life will be godly.   [918

TITHING
You cannot get around it; the scripture promises material and spiritual benefits to the man who gives to God. You cannot out-give God. I challenge you to try it and see. [919

... Blessings. We have found in our own home, as have thousands of others, that God's blessings upon the nine-tenths, when we tithe, helps it to go farther than ten-tenths without His blessing. [920

TOLERANCE

In some ways, Jesus was one of the most tolerant of all men; and yet when it came to sin and salvation, He was extremely narrow. [921

... Sins, Sinners. Jesus was intolerant toward sin. He was tolerant toward the sinner, but intolerant toward the evil which enslaved him. [922

... When Harmful. The popular, tolerant attitude toward the Gospel of Christ is like a man going to watch the Dodgers and the Braves play a baseball game and rooting for both sides. It would be impossible for a man who has no pledged loyalty to a particular team to really get into the game. [923

TRADITION

Christian faith is often in conflict with tradition. Jesus' greatest concern was with the Pharisees, who were motivated not by love, but by regard for their traditions. [924

TRANSGRESSION

... Sinful Thinking. All transgression begins with sinful thinking. You who have come to Christ for a pure heart, guard against the pictures of lewdness and sensuality which satan flashes upon the screen of your imaginations, select with care the books you read, choose discerningly the kind of entertainment you attend, the kind of associates with whom you mingle, and the kind of environment in which you place yourself. You should no more allow sinful imaginations to accumulate in your mind and soul than you would let garbage collect in your living room. [925

TRINITY

The Bible teaches us that God is in Three Persons. God is One, but He is manifested in Three Persons. God the Father, God the Son, and God the Holy Spirit. Don't ask me to explain it—I can't. It's impossible for me to explain to you the Holy Trinity. I accept it by faith. God the Father; God the Son, who is equal with the Father in every respect; God the Holy Spirit, who is equal with the Son and with the Father in every respect. [926

TRUTH

We can win the hearts of nations by truth, righteousness and justice. [927

... **Contrary.** By words, looks, and actions men design to make an impression that is contrary to the truth. [928

... **Timeliness.** Truth is timeless. Truth does not differ from one age to another, from one people to another, from one geographical location to another. Men's ideas may differ, men's customs may change, men's moral codes may vary, but the great, all-prevailing truth stands for time and eternity. [929

... **Word Of God.** The truth is the Word of God. We are to be girded and undergirded with the Word. [930

··U··

UNCONCERN

...Apathy. What makes us Christians shrug our shoulders when we ought to be flexing our muscles? What makes us apathetic in a day when there are loads to lift, a world to be won and captives to be set free? Why are so many bored when the times demand action? Christ told us that in the last days there would be an insipid attitude toward life. [931

UNDERSTANDING

...Faith. I do not understand the digestive system, but I eat. I don't understand all about our respiratory system, but I continue to breathe. So it is with faith. We cannot understand all things. We must have faith.   [932

UNFAITHFULNESS

Unfaithfulness, too, is an enemy of the home. Mr. Kinsey believed, as a result of his exhaustive study, that "about half of all married males" have been guilty of unfaithfulness. Many others admitted that they would have been unfaithful, but for fear of social disapproval. This tragic knowledge has served to aggravate the situation rather than to solve the problem.   [933

UNITY

We are living examples of a misuse of the concept "in unity there is strength and in individuality there is weakness."   [934

UNREST

In my travels about the country, I have sensed unrest in almost every phase of our modern-day living.   [935

URGENCY

If there was ever a time when we should man the lifeboats and go out and rescue as many as we can, it is now.   [936

In talking with Christian leaders, I feel a new sense of urgency among them. There is an air of expectancy and an awareness of impending crisis.   [937

· · V · ·

VENEREAL DISEASE

... **America.** Venereal disease has reached epidemic proportions throughout much of America, and all this in the face of the latest in contraceptives and antibiotics.   [938

... **Judgment.** Those who scoff at the idea of judgment would do well to study the latest statistics on illegitimate births and venereal diseases.   [939

VERTIGO

... **Spiritual.** If a pilot takes his eyes off the instrument panel, he suffers what is called vertigo. He begins to depend on his reasoning and feelings. He has a tendency to turn the plane. It feels like it's going left when actually it's going right. And there are thousands of people today who are suffering from spiritual vertigo. They've gotten their eyes off the instrument panel. They go by their own reasoning. They have figured out what Christianity is within their personal philosophy of life. They plan to get to heaven their own way. But they are going to crash on the rocks, or in the water, or into a mountain. They are headed for destruction. If you are one of these persons, you're going to end up in hell because of vertigo. The instrument panel is the Bible, the Holy Scripture, and when you go against the instructions of this book, you're suffering from spiritual vertigo even though you may be sincere.   [940

VICTORY

From the divine viewpoint the defeated Christian is a monstrosity. He is abnormal. If you as a Christian are overcome by the enemy, the simple explanation is that Christ has been denied His rightful position of supremacy in your heart. It is Christ, and Christ alone, who can give you a constant, daily victorious life.   [941

$\cdot\ \cdot\ W\ \cdot\ \cdot$

WAR

   ... Civilization. I visited the Auca Indians in Ecuador, and there I found people living in the Stone Age. I saw them lying, cheating, hating, killing. War has almost completely annihilated the various tribes of the Auca Indians. I said to myself, "What these people need is education, economic security, better food, better clothes." It is true that they need them all. But when I come to New York and Paris and London and Moscow, what do I find? People who have all of these advantages, and who are still lying, hating, cheating and killing. The most devastating wars of history have been fought by the so-called civilized countries.   [942

   ... Korea. In the front lines of Korea, I never saw a pinup picture. But I saw hundreds of Bibles.   [943

   ... Peace. Until we solve the human equation called man and get him straightened out, we will never have a peaceful world. You've got to be better men before you can have a better society.   [944

WARFARE

   ... Spiritual. Consciously or unconsciously the entire

country is engaged at this hour in a mighty, tremendous, spiritual warfare. [945

WEALTH

...**Bible.** In the Bible Jesus had a lot to say about the rich. There's nothing wrong with being rich. Some of the greatest men of the Bible were rich. But it's what we do with our riches that God is going to look at, and our motives, and our intent. [946

...**God's Gift.** John D. Rockefeller made his millions in oil, but if a benevolent God had not put the oil in the ground, and hadn't endowed man with the sense to refine it and market it, there would be no fortunes in oil. [947

...**Possessions.** There is nothing wrong with men possessing riches. The wrong comes when riches possess men. [948

WESTERN WORLD

...**Christianity.** One hundred years ago 25 per cent of those in the Western world were Christian—at least in name. If the present trend continues, by 1990 it is estimated that less than 10 per cent of the entire Western world will profess faith in the name of Jesus Christ. [949

...**Dilemma.** By its rejection of orthodox Christianity, the Western world now has no philosophy and no intellectual framework to combat communism. [950

WITNESSING

Your lips must become the lips of the resurrected Christ,

to speak His messages, to be His witness. This means that the harsh, unkind words remain unspoken.   [951

WIVES

. . . Suggestions to.   I have some suggestions that are not in the Bible that I want to give to wives. When your husband comes home in the evening, even though you have been working all day, I would suggest that you run to meet him at the door with a kiss. Keep his love at any cost. Be attractive.   [952

WOMEN

. . . Equality.   I do not think that the Bible in any way teaches that women are inferior. The Apostle Paul made a statement about women to the effect that they should be quiet. I believe the reason he said it was because in the synagogues of that day, women would sit in the balcony—as in some parts of the world today, and would talk so loudly that the rest of the people could not hear the speaker. So Paul said, let the women be quiet. That did not mean they were inferior.   [953

. . . Influence.   Women have tremendous influence on a man. You young women who are thinking about getting married, remember this—physical attraction is part of it, mental affinity is part of it, spiritual oneness is most of it.   [954

. . . Status; Dignity.   Down through the centuries, in every society, there have been some things that men have naturally done and other things that women have done. But it was Christianity that freed the woman from her subservient role. And I have never understood how a woman could reject Christ, for it was Christ who gave dignity to women. He elevated their status. [955

WORLD

...Basic Problem. The basic problem facing our world is not just social inequity, lack of education, or even physical hunger. We are finding that highly educated and well-fed people have greeds, hate, passion and lust that are not eliminated by any known process of education . . . The roots of sin in our hearts are extremely deep and this is the basic cause of the world's problems—and only the fire of the Lord can burn them out. [956

...Condition Of. Today some like to find consolation in the fact that the world appears to be going on well, if not smoothly. There is marrying and giving in marriage. There is business, the professions, education, entertainment, etc. But these in no way nullify the threat of the world's end. They are but evidences of the fact mankind is marking time. [957

...Destruction Of. I believe the earth will be consumed by fire, not only because God said it, but because science has created weapons that can do it. [958

...End Of. God is the sovereign of the world as it now is. Man has defaced it, and in His own good time God will bring history to an end. Even science is ready to acknowledge that the end of the world in the near future is more than a remote possibility. [959

Jesus talked about the end of the world system and the establishment of a kingdom of righteousness. Christ did not engage in fantasy. He was not given to terror tactics. He was truth and veracity personified. He warned, "When you see certain things coming to pass, you can be assured that the end is very near." [960

We dare not forget that the world is approaching an end-time, that there is a hell to escape and a heaven to gain.[961

...Enemies. There are storms in the world today: storms of unbelief, materialism, secularism, moral degeneracy and international difficulties. And there are storms in your own life. [962

...Its Values. One of the reasons why the Bible warns us to "Love not the world, neither the things in the world," is that the world's values are constantly changing. [963

...Missionaries. There is coming a day when instead of our sending missionaries to India and Africa, they may well be sending missionaries to us. [964

...Modern Generation. This generation has been called "the tormented generation." Certainly this is the generation destined to live in the midst of crisis, danger, fear, war, and death. [965

...Need. The greatest need in the world today is not more powerful man-made weapons but men and women to be born again by the Holy Spirit, by repenting of their sins and receiving Christ as Savior, and using the power of their conversion to help save the entire world.   [966

... **Problem.** The problem of the world is not the hydrogen bomb, or even communism. The problem is depraved human nature . . . There is no difference in the nature of a savage walking a jungle trail with a spear in his hand and an educated, cultured American flying a bomber overhead.   [967

... **Reality.** Generally speaking, the world dislikes to face reality and most certainly dislikes change.   [968

... **Religion.** "Is Religion Big Enough to Save the World?" That question could be answered very simply. If the world could be saved by religion it would have been saved long ago.   [969

... **Situation.** The world situation is so critical that even scientists and philosophers are sounding words of alarm. And some of them are calling upon the country and the world to turn back to God.   [970

WORLD LEADERSHIP

... **America.** Many people of the world think of us as a nation of gangsters, all of us filthy rich, only interested in pleasure and fun, but there is another side to America that sometimes they do not see. America at the moment has taken a position of world leadership. Now the question that many people around the world are asking is if we have the moral leadership to direct the free world. I feel a revival of true

Christian faith in America would do more to give us this moral leadership than anything that we could do.   [971

WORLDLINESS

Today, in what we call the society of the world, we hold spiritual things in contempt and lust after the things of this world.   [972

Worldliness is a spirit, an atmosphere, an influence, permeating the whole of life in human society, and it needs to be guarded against constantly and strenuously.   [973

. . . Godliness. There are two worlds: The world that we measure with instruments, and the world that we know with our hearts and imaginations. Worldliness is one way of life; Godliness is another, and the two don't mix. Worldliness has the things of this world as its goal. Godliness has the things of eternity as its goal. The one is the short view; the other is the long view.   [974

WORLD RELIGIONS

Many of the world's religions appeal to a particular race of people or nationality. Mohammedanism makes its appeal to the Arab world. Hinduism appeals largely to the Indian mind. Buddhism is slanted to the Oriental philosophy. But the appeal of the cross of Christ is universal.   [975

WORRY

There is no use telling people not to worry when they have just cause for worry. I am not of that school of philosophy which glibly proclaims: "Smile, and the world smiles with you; weep and you weep alone."   [976

...Results Of. Worry is more adept than Father Time in etching deep lines into the face. It is disastrous to health, robs life of its zest, crowds out constructive, creative thinking, and cripples the soul.   [977

WRITERS

...Pessimism. Because the authors do not believe in life after death, the writings of this generation are filled with tragedy and pessimism. The writings of William Faulkner, James Joyce, Ernest Hemingway, Eugene O'Neill, and many others are filled with pessimism, darkness, and tragedy.   [978

·· Y ··

YOUNG PEOPLE

...Insecurity. Today's young people cannot make plans
as our generation made them. Theirs is a different era, an
era filled with danger and menaced by storm clouds on the
horizon. Unless we solve the problems of our generation the
world may be blown up. We do not have any more time. We
cannot wait any longer. That is why our young people are
restless. They are afraid. They are insecure, and they are
marching and searching and rebelling.   [979

...Suggestions To Live By. Ten suggestions for young
people to live by:

1. Avoid the wrong company.
2. Watch your eyes. You cannot help the first look, but
you can help the second look. Job said: "I will make a
covenant with my eyes, why then shall I look upon a
maid?"
3. Watch your lips. The Bible says evil communications
can corrupt your life. Refrain from telling dirty or off-color
stories.
4. Watch your heart. This carries with it the idea of
imagination. Don't let evil thoughts stay in your mind.
5. Watch your dress. I know a girl who always dressed
provocatively until she was converted to Christ Jesus.

Now she says: "I dress as though Christ were my escort each evening."

6. Watch your recreation and amusements. Be careful about the films and TV shows you watch. Choose only the highest and the best.

7. Be careful what you read. The newsstands are filled today with pornographic literature. Avoid them like the plague; they stimulate evil passions.

8. Watch your idleness. When David was idle on the top of his house, he saw Bathsheba and took her to him. Too much leisure and idleness for young people is harmful in many ways.

9. Have Christ in your heart and life. Joseph had such strong religious convictions that, even though it might have meant death, he refused to be immoral with Potiphar's wife.

10. Take a delight in the Word of God. The Bible says: "Thy word have I hid in my heart, that I might not sin against Thee."   [980

YOUTH

One-half of the population of the U. S. today is under 25 years of age and by 1970 it will be 60%. The cult of our youth is on the way to dominating our total society. All America is in a race to see who can look, act, and be the swingingest and who can live and look the youngest. We see it in the cars we buy, the clothes we wear, the books and magazines we read, the movies, the Lolitas, the sex kittens, the Candys and the Pussycats. Everybody is trying to act young when what we need is maturity in leading youth along the right path.   [981

. . . Adult. Instead of casting a critical eye at our young people, it would be better for adults to stop and think what kind of a world we have built for our young people to live in. It is a world so full of tension and strife that it is difficult enough for grownups, much less youth, to feel secure. [982

. . . Alcohol And Narcotics. Young people get caught in alcohol and narcotics, just as they get caught in sex experiences—not because they want to do it. Everything inside them tells them that they shouldn't, but everybody else is doing it, and they would be considered an odd ball, a square. [983

. . . Answer To Problems. There are thousands of young people who have found a cure for the frustrations and contradictions of adolescence. They have discovered an answer to the problems of boredom and insecurity and sex, through accepting Jesus Christ and His way of life. They have found a peace, a security, a happiness, a zest in living. [984

. . . Authority. Although many do not realize it, youth demands authority. Many parents and teachers fail to realize that youth responds to rules, regulations and discipline.[985

. . . Challenge. I have found in our Crusades throughout the world, that young people will respond if the challenge is tough enough and hard enough. [986

. . . Energy. Youth is full of energy, and if that energy is not used in constructive ways, it will be used in harmful and dangerous ways. Being a dedicated Christian takes these sources of youthful energy and converts them to useful, constructive purposes. [987

... Failure Of Church. All too often young people get the idea that the church is a place for complicated theological disputes, where they hear reams of statistics—poor quality of Sunday School teaching—and the lack of an authoritative, challenging message. Much of what goes on in the church is often over the heads of young people. We have failed to talk straight from the shoulder to young people about their problems, such as sex, obedience to parents, honesty, Christianity. [988

... Going Steady. Difficulty arises when young people start going steady too early; problems arise in the control of feelings. There is danger of too much intimacy. And then when a breakup occurs someone is going to get hurt. [989

... Lawlessness. Lawlessness among youth is rampant, immorality accepted, and disobedience to all laws and rules is thought smart. Parents, educators and police officers are standing helplessly on the side, not knowing which way to turn. [990

... Leadership. Young people want leadership and direction. They want a master and a controller. Actually, they were built for God, and without God as the center of their lives they become frustrated and confused, desperately grasping and searching for security. [991

217

... Petting. Heavy petting should be reserved for marriage. Heavy petting stimulates your urges and can weaken your moral strengths as well as being destructive to the body and the spirit. [992

... Pressure. Young people are being pressured too much. The pressure begins by the time they are ten years of age. They go to formal dances at ten, have steady dates at 13, and drive their own cars at 16. They are in college by the time they are 17, already satiated and jaded by life. [993

... Questions. The great questions on the modern university campuses today are: Where did I come from? Why am I here? Where am I going? and what is the reason for my existence? [994

... Rebels. We've got some young rebels today that I want to shake up a little bit. I'd like to shave them, cut their hair, bathe them and then preach to them. [995

... Revolt Against The Church. Young people are in revolt against institutional Christianity. They are not in revolt against God; they are not in revolt against Christ; they are in revolt against the church. [996

... Revolt, Europe. While we were in Denmark to conduct an evangelistic crusade, we were amazed at the young people. It was difficult to tell the boys from the girls, because nearly all the boys had long hair down to their shoulders. The young people of Northern Europe are in revolt. They are in revolt against their parents' generation. [997

· · Z · ·

ZEAL

Every Christian should become an ambassador of Christ with the splendid madness and gay abandon of Francis of Assisi. Every Christian should be so intoxicated with Christ and so filled with holy fervor that nothing could ever quench his ardor.   [998

... **Disciples.** Think of the glorious daring of Christ's men! Paul was satisfied with nothing less than taking the Gospel to Rome, to Spain, to any place the Lord sent him. John Wesley set out to preach Christ to the whole world. These men had a magnificent obsession. Fired by such fervor and inspired by such an enterprise, who could withstand their zeal? They carried the flaming truths of the Gospel far and wide, reckoning nothing of peril, persecution and reproach. They surmounted obstacles, overcame difficulties and endured persecution. That was their madness, the madness of doing great things for God.   [999

... **Victory.** If you are a Christian, there is no excuse for not having daily victory in your life by renouncing sin and by faith letting the Spirit of God have control of your life.

But to you who are "natural" men, you who have never known the joy and peace that Jesus gives, you can, by turning from your sin and by faith accepting Christ as Lord and Savior, be forgiven, and you can know the peace with God that only Christ can bring. Why not turn to Him right now? [1,000

Index

CHILDREN (Also see Parents)
—648;
Church—91;
Father—313;
Juvenile Delinquency—93;
Obedience; Discipline—94; 245;
Obedience to Parents—95;
Parental Authority—96;
Parents; Counseling—97;
Respect—98;
Spoiling—99;
Understanding—100;

CHOICE—324; 883;

CHRIST—101;
Acceptance—102;
Birth—141; 142; 143;
Blood Of—103;
Church—104;
Coming—105;
His Message—106;
How to Receive Him—107;
Injustice; Prejudice—108;
Perfection—109;
Power—110; 111;
Second Coming—809; 810;
811; 812;
Sin, Cure For—112;
Truth—113;
Victorious—114;

CHRISTIAN—54; 530; 536; 577;
905; 912; 924;
Discipline—115;
Education—116;
Holy Life; Example—117;
Strength—118;

CHRISTIANITY—418; 638;
693; 733; 741; 770; 821;
949;
Applied—119;

CHRISTIANITY (Continued)
Caricature—120;
Definition—121;
Exclusivity—122;
Satisfaction—123;
Victory—124;

CHRISTIAN LIFE
Conflict—125;
Difficulty—126;
Power Of—127;
Realities—128;
Rules For—784;
Worldly Life—129;

CHRISTIANS—677; 898; 937;
Action—130;
Business—131;
Compromise—187;
Example—132;
Giving—332;
Life—133;
Modern Life—134;
Mothers—135;
Pleasure—136;
Prohibitions—137;
Sincerity—138;
Worldliness—139; 140;

CHRISTMAS—141; 142; 143;
330;
Meaning—144;

CHURCH—104; 414; 508; 645;
646; 672; 676; 742; 775;
808;
Attendance—145; 146; 147;
Attitude Toward—148;
Children—91;
Church-Goers—149;
Comfort—150;
Concern—151;
Definition—152;
Denomination—153;

· · Y · ·

· · Z · ·

A Brief Chronological History of the
Billy Graham Crusades

"A crusade is a continuing thing; a campaign is more just a part of a crusade. A crusade goes on and on and is world wide in its ramifications."

* * * * *

1949—LOS ANGELES, CALIFORNIA

The first crusade called an "evangelistic campaign," was held in Charlotte, N. C., in November 1947. It was followed by campaigns in 1948 and 1949 in Augusta, Ga., Modesto, Calif., Miami, Fla., Baltimore, Md. and Altoona, Pa. But it was the campaign held in a canvas tent at the corner of Washington Boulevard and Hill Street in Los Angeles, in September of 1949 that brought Billy Graham to national prominence. The tent would hold only 6,000 people and even that was too large a capacity for the crowds that came to hear the 30 year old evangelist and his Team: Cliff Barrows, George Beverly Shea and Grady Wilson. The crowds began to increase by the end of the scheduled three weeks, and a last minute decision extended the crusade to six weeks. By the end of that time, Billy Graham had received not only local fame, but also national publicity for his evangelism.

1949-1950—BOSTON, MASSACHUSETTS

Committed to an "evangelistic campaign" in Boston, the crusade Team began its meetings in the Park Street Congregational

Church. Overwhelmingly large crowds forced a shift to Mechanics Hall but even this was not large enough. Thanks to the efforts of the Catholic editor of the *Boston Post,* the final meeting was held in Boston Garden where more than 16,000 people attended. Billy Graham returned to Boston on April 23. At his outdoor Peace Rally on Monument Hill, the police estimated that almost 50,000 were present.

It was after this second visit to Boston on July 14, 1950 that Billy Graham was first invited to the White House. There he and the Team had a twenty-minute talk with President Harry S Truman, followed by a prayer.

1950—COLUMBIA, SOUTH CAROLINA

Columbia (the capital of South Carolina) was the first place the term "crusade" was used rather than "campaign." It began on February 19th at Township Auditorium, which held only 4,000 persons. It ended on March 12 in the football stadium of the University of South Carolina where a crowd of 40,000 packed the stands. The governor of the state and other dignitaries attended. Billy Graham's Team was expanded in Columbia in preparation for crusades to come.

1950—PORTLAND, OREGON

The Portland Crusade was held in an aluminum Auditorium temporarily constructed by the crusade committee to hold 20,000 people. It was at this crusade that the idea of a national radio program was presented to Billy Graham by Walter Bennett and Fred Dienert. One night after the regular collection had been taken up, Dr. Graham told the crowd of the broadcast plans—if $25,000 could be raised to pay for the first four weeks time. Before midnight the money was in hand to begin what was to become "The Hour of Decision" radio program—a name chosen by Mrs. Ruth Graham. This twenty-five thousand dollars led to the decision to establish The Billy Graham Evangelistic Association, a non-profit organization. George Wilson flew out to Portland with the papers of incorporation, and on his return to Minneapolis set up a one-room office and hired one secretary, just in case the proposed radio program drew any mail.

(That one-room office, with one secretary and no budget, has grown to an organization now operating eight offices on four continents and employing nearly a thousand persons, including 400 in Minneapolis; with George Wilson as executive vice-president and treasurer).

The Portland Crusade was followed by the Minneapolis, Minn. Crusade in September.

1950—ATLANTA, GEORGIA

The Atlanta Crusade was held in a specially constructed tabernacle on the baseball field of the Atlanta Crackers at Ponce de Leon Park. There, on Sunday November 5th, "The Hour of Decision" was first broadcast over 150 stations on the ABC radio network. (In five weeks it had earned the highest audience rating ever accorded a religious program. Within five years it was heard weekly on a total of 850 stations around the world).

1951—FORT WORTH, TEXAS

It was at the Fort Worth Crusade that the "follow up" system of counselors was inaugurated by the Team, so that the wave of religious emotion created by mass evangelism would not evaporate once the crusade had ended. It was also at Fort Worth that the first Billy Graham feature film (World Wide Pictures) "Mr. Texas," based on the actual decision of a Texas cowboy, was produced.

1951—SHREVEPORT, LOUISIANA

This crusade began in a 3,000 seat auditorium and had to be shifted to the 17,000 seat baseball stadium. Here it was proven (by the increased attendance) that non-church people will come more readily to an open air meeting. Thereafter, climate and circumstances permitting, the crusades have been held in stadiums.

1952—WASHINGTON, D. C.

Following crusades in Seattle, in August, and Hollywood, in September 1951, the five week crusade in Washington, D. C. was held in the National Guard Armory in January, 1952. An act of Congress instigated by Speaker of the House Sam Rayburn permitted an unusual service to be held on the steps of the Capitol where Billy Graham read Lincoln's 1863 proclamation for a day of humiliation and prayer, and followed it with a short stirring prayer of his own that the nation return to God, the Bible, the Church. The service was carried nationwide on radio and television.

1952—HOUSTON, TEXAS

The Houston Crusade produced the second World Wide Pictures feature film, "Oiltown—USA." It told the story of the conversion experience of a millionaire oilman. The Houston Crusade was followed by crusades in Jackson, Miss., Pittsburgh, Pa., and Albuquerque, N. M.

1953—CHATTANOOGA, TENNESSEE

On March 15th, 1953 (more than a year before the famous Supreme Court decision of May 17, 1954) Billy Graham and the Team opened their first deliberately integrated crusade in the southern city of Chattanooga, Tennessee. Billy Graham insisted that Negroes be allowed to sit anywhere they wanted in the civic auditorium.

1953—DALLAS, TEXAS

Following a successful crusade in St. Louis, Billy Graham and the Team went to Dallas. In the Dallas Crusade (during May and June) segregated seating returned by decision of the local crusade committee—but Billy Graham made his personal feelings against segregation known by refusing to ride up to his hotel room in an elevator unless a Negro friend could go with him. The Dallas Crusade was followed by those in Syracuse, Detroit, and Asheville, N. C.

1954—GREATER LONDON CRUSADE

Arriving in London, England, in February, 1954, Billy Graham was met by a hostile press. There was great concern that Harringay Arena (which held 12,000) would not only not be full for the opening of the crusade, but that the crowd might be very sparse indeed. But despite inclement weather, the stadium was filled and 178 persons came forward at the end of his sermon. Except for the second night (due to snow flurries and rain), there was never an empty seat in the stadium during the three months of the crusade.

On April 3rd, in Trafalgar Square, the largest crowd since "V. E. Day" heard Billy Graham speak. And on April 16th, more than 40,000 crowded into Hyde Park to hear him preach.

The last day of the Greater London Crusade, Billy Graham spoke to 120,000 persons in Wembley Stadium—the greatest religious congregation ever seen until then in the British Isles. During the three months of the crusade more than 38,000 persons had "come forward" to make their decision for Christ.

Before leaving London Billy Graham was summoned to 10 Downing Street for a forty-minute interview with the British Prime Minister, Sir Winston Churchill. He returned to America to find that the original hostile furor in the British press, plus his later triumphs there, had made him a household word throughout the United States. In the Fall of 1954, crusades were conducted in Nashville and New Orleans.

1955—ALL SCOTLAND CRUSADE

For the first time the crusade came to the British Isles with the official endorsement of the churches. Held in Kevin Hall, in

Glasgow, Scotland, the peak of the All Scotland Crusade was the Good Friday television and radio broadcast over the BBC to the whole of the United Kingdom. It was viewed by an audience second in number only to that which watched the Coronation of Queen Elizabeth II.

1955—WEMBLEY LONDON

Billy Graham and his Team had never before returned to a city for a second crusade, and no stadium the size of Wembley had ever been taken for so long a time as seven nights. Between 50,000 and 60,000 people attended every night, with about 3,000 inquirers coming forward at each service. The Sunday following the close of the Crusade Billy Graham was invited by the Queen to preach to the Royal Family in the Royal Chapel at Windsor Great Park.

1955—PARIS

The Paris Crusade lasted five days and was the first crusade at which Billy Graham preached using an interpreter to translate his words to the great crowds. The Paris Crusade was followed by a whirlwind tour of twelve cities in Switzerland, West Germany, Scandinavia and Holland.

1955—TORONTO

The first Canadian Crusade was held for three weeks in Toronto. It was at this crusade that the hymn *How Great Thou Art,* conducted by Cliff Barrows and sung by George Beverly Shea and the Toronto Crusade Choir was first used by the crusade; the start of what was to become the most popular hymn in North America.

1955—CAMBRIDGE (University) England

Having accepted an invitation by Cambridge's Inter-Collegiate Christian Union, a controversial undergraduate religious body, Billy Graham returned to England in the summer of 1955.

Services were held for a week in the ancient University Church. He spoke to students and a group of Chaplains and members of the theological faculty who at best were neutral, and at worst a highly critical audience. Feeling he was pandering to the intellect of the group and not getting through to them, Billy Graham threw away his prepared sermons and preached once again as if he were before the most ordinary audience, and at last reached them.

1956—INDIA AND FAR EAST

In Bombay crowds at each meeting of the crusade were of a size unprecedented for a Christian minister. Public interest seemed almost as great among Hindus as it was among the Christian minority. At Madras, every sentence Billy Graham preached was translated twice, into Telegu and Tamil. The crusade in India lasted almost four weeks. En route back to the United States, one-day meetings were held in Manila, Hong Kong, Formosa, Japan, Korea and Hawaii. On his return, Billy Graham went immediately to Washington and made strong representations on India's behalf to President Dwight Eisenhower. Eisenhower said of him at a press conference: "He carries his religion to the far corners of the earth, trying to promote mediation instead of conflict, tolerance instead of prejudice."

It was in 1956 that the Rev. T. W. Wilson, brother of Grady Wilson, joined the Team. Crusades in Richmond, Va., Oklahoma City and Louisville, Ky., closed out the year.

1957—NEW YORK CITY

From the start, the New York Crusade (held at Madison Square Garden) broke all records for attendance, for decisions, for impact on a city. During this crusade the idea of a televised announcement giving a local telephone number to call for counseling was first devised and used. It was the first nationally televised crusade in history. Ethel Waters, the famous Negro blues singer and actress, first joined the choir and later sang as a solo her famous hit song from a Broadway play, *His Eye Is On The Sparrow*. She has visited crusades ever since, at her own expense "to sing for Billy." At the closing rally of the New York Crusade, 100,000 persons packed Yankee Stadium on July 20. Another 20,000 outside the gates listened over loudspeakers. This remains the largest crowd in Yankee Stadium history.

Vice-President Nixon brought a message from President Eisenhower and addressed the crowd before Graham's sermon. The crusade was then extended beyond the July 20th date and ran for a total of sixteen weeks. It ended with a rally in Times Square on the evening of September 1st. The total attendance was 2,357,400, the highest for any event in the history of Madison Square Garden, and the number of decisions (apart from those of telecast viewers) was 61,148.

1958—CENTRAL AMERICA

The three-week crusade to the Caribbean and Central America had lasting significance over and above the countries visited, due to the time spent in perfecting the principles of counseling and follow-up to long-term missionary evangelism which finally evolved into "Evangelism in Depth."

1958—SAN FRANCISCO, CALIFORNIA

The San Francisco Crusade lasted from April 27 to June 22 and was one of the most successful crusades ever. Night after night the vast Cow Palace was filled and those who came forward to make decisions included members of the famous San Francisco Giant baseball team and other great Bay Area athletes.

1958—CHARLOTTE, NORTH CAROLINA

In 1958 Billy Graham returned to Charlotte for a crusade in his native state of North Carolina. More Negroes attended than at any time since Graham had stopped segregated crusades. On the evening after the Charlotte Crusade ended Graham held the first non-segregated mass meeting in South Carolina history at Fort Jackson military base, after the governor had refused to allow Graham to use the statehouse grounds in Columbia. Sixty thousand whites and Negroes attended.

1959—MELBOURNE, AUSTRALIA

Because Australia was known for not taking kindly to evangelists—especially foreign evangelists—the Melbourne Crusade started on February 15th in the Festival Hall, an indoor arena that seated only 10,000. After five days it had to move to the outdoor Sidney Myer Music Bowl where crowds of up to 70,000 attended nightly. The final meeting of the crusade on March 15th was held in the Melbourne Cricket Ground where the total admission announced by the Secretary of the Melbourne Cricket Club was 143,750. There were 28,105 decisions for Christ recorded at the Melbourne Crusade.

1959—NEW ZEALAND

After the Melbourne Crusade ended, Billy Graham and the Team went to Tasmania for two one-night meetings and then opened his New Zealand Crusade in Auckland (New Zealand's largest city) on March 29. In the four-day, three-city crusade—two days at Auckland, and one each at Wellington and Christchurch—over twenty percent of New Zealand's total population attended the meetings.

1959—SYDNEY, AUSTRALIA

Sydney was the first place where a campaign was waged to have every home in the city visited by a church member, bringing to every citizen an invitation to attend the crusade. Called "a city of happy pagans," Sydney turned out in mass at the Royal Agricultural Society's Showgrounds for the weeks of the crusade which ended on May 10th with 150,000 people in the Showground and the adjoining Cricket Ground, linked together by amplifiers. At the end of the sermon on May 10th, 5,683 people came forward. On his return to the U. S., crusades were held that Fall in Wheaton, Ill., and Indianapolis, Ind.

1960—AFRICA

The Africa Crusade lasted from January to March, avoiding the Union of South Africa, although invited by the churches to come. In Ethiopia, Emperor Haile Selassie turned over the Royal Stadium to the Team for the crusade, and had a ninety minute meeting with Billy Graham. A color movie *Africa on the Bridge,* made by Dick Ross of the crusade's World Wide Pictures, later won a Golden Reel award for Documentary in 1960.

Following the Africa Crusade, Billy Graham conducted his second successful crusade in Washington, D. C.

1960—SWITZERLAND AND GERMANY

After a three-week crusade in Berne, Basel and Lausanne, plus two days in Zurich, the Billy Graham Team went to West Germany for three crusades, the most historical of which was a week in Berlin where the great tent was pitched at the Brandenburg Gate; and the final meeting was held in the open in front of the Reichstag.

In November 1960 after his return to the states from the Germany Crusade the first monthly edition of *Decision Magazine* was published by the Evangelistic Association. The magazine is edited by Dr. Sherwood Eliot Wirt, a Presbyterian pastor from Oakland, California, and author of the book, *Crusade at the Golden Gate.* (*Decision* was a success from the first issue and now has a circulation of over 3,000,000 both in America and foreign countries. The circulation is the highest of any religious periodical in America.)

In October, 1960, a "Spanish Crusade" was held in New York City.

1961—MIAMI, FLORIDA

There were five crusades in 1961, starting with a Florida tour in January and February.

The Miami Crusade in March, reached not only tourists and native Floridians but Cuban refugees and vacationing students. The mayor of Fort Lauderdale sent a message to Billy Graham to come address thousands of rowdy students who had invaded the beach area. Standing on a wooden platform, his back to the sea, Billy Graham overcame the initial catcalls of the students and preached for an hour to the most rapt audience that had ever listened to him.

1961—MANCHESTER, ENGLAND

The Team returned to England in May, 1961, where the Manchester Council of Churches declined to cooperate. For the first week of the crusade, Billy Graham was ill in London with a throat infection and high temperature. Leighton Ford substituted to preach to crowds larger than the ones in London's Harringay arena. Billy Graham arrived for the second and third weeks, although still a sick man, and the crusade gained even more momentum with tens of thousands of people standing in the rain to hear him. In July, the Fresno, Calif. Crusade was launched.

1961—PHILADELPHIA, PENNSYLVANIA

When the Team returned to the U. S., a crusade was held in Minneapolis (July), followed by the Philadelphia Crusade in August. The Philadelphia Crusade was important in that the first "seminars in evangelism" began there—a full-scale seminar of lectures in preparation for carrying out of the crusade. It was to become an invaluable part of future crusades.

1962—CHICAGO, ILLINOIS

The Chicago Crusade was held in the New McCormick Place. Every night for three months the 40,000 seats were filled.

The crusade ended with 116,000 persons in attendance at Soldiers Field Stadium. Because the TV film of the crusade was seven minutes short, Billy Graham returned to the empty stadium that night, and sitting there alone on the platform he spoke directly to the television audience, producing one of the most dramatic impacts ever witnessed on American television, causing letters to pour in from all over the country.

1962—SOUTH AMERICA

The South America Crusade was divided into two parts—Jan.–Feb. and Sept.–Oct., 1962—and included meetings in Montevideo, Paraguay; Sao Paulo, Brazil; and Buenos Aires, Argentina—all held in the largest stadiums in these great South American cities.

On his return in October 1962, Billy Graham unknowingly was carrying a rare bacillus, and had to be hospitalized in January 1963, but he nevertheless flew to Washington for the Presidential Prayer Breakfast. After addressing the gathering, he went with President Kennedy to talk a few moments to the wives of the ambassadors and senators, and on with the President to his limousine for a lengthy talk.

In November a crusade was conducted in El Paso, Texas.

1963—LOS ANGELES, CALIFORNIA

In 1963, after crusades in Paris, Nuremberg and Stuttgart the Team returned to Los Angeles where Billy Graham had first sprung to fame fourteen years before, but this time it was at the invitation of the Southern California Council of Churches, which involved 3,500 individual churches, 7,000 trained counselors and advisers, and a choir that numbered from 3,000 to 5,000.

The whole Graham Team was at Los Angeles including the nucleus that began it all in 1949: Billy Graham, Grady Wilson, Cliff Barrows and George Beverly Shea supported by the eleven other associate and staff evangelists, including Akbar Haqq from India, and Fernando Vangioni from Latin America. Instead of a canvas tent the crusade was held in the Los Angeles Coliseum, and on the final night 134,254 people entered the stadium—the largest number ever recorded for any event at America's largest stadium. On one "youth night" alone, 3,216 came forward, the largest number ever to make a decision in one night in America.

1964–65—THE WORLD'S FAIR

The New York World's Fair opened in April, 1964 and included the Billy Graham Pavilion. Designed by the noted architect Edward Durell Stone, the central feature was a wide-screen film theater showing a specially prepared film called *Man in the Fifth Dimension*. In keeping with the theme of the Fair, the film looked at the marvels of the universe and life, with Billy Graham as guide, discussing man's rebellion against his Creator and the way of reconciliation through Christ. In the two-year period of the Fair, more than 5,000,000 persons, from 125 countries, visited the Pavilion. More than one million saw the film, and thousands remained for counseling.

1964—BOSTON, MASSACHUSETTS

Two of the most memorable crusades of 1964 were in Boston—one in the summer and one in the fall. At the beginning of the first crusade, Cardinal Cushing, the Roman Catholic prelate of the Boston Archdiocese, issued a statement of welcome to the evangelist and his Team. During the second crusade, Billy Graham sent a message asking for an appointment with Cardinal Cushing, to express his gratitude; and, when he reached the Cardinal's house on the appointed morning, found a full battery of reporters, television and news cameras and radio microphones, arranged for by the Catholic prelate. For forty-five minutes the Cardinal and the evangelist conversed in public on such subjects as the Ecumenical Council in Rome, of a common translation of the Bible, and of Pope John and Pope Paul.

Crusades were also held in Phoenix, Ariz., San Diego, Canada, Columbus, Ohio, and Omaha, Neb.

1965—COPENHAGEN, DENMARK

One of the most difficult crusades ever held was in Copenhagen, Denmark. It was particularly significant because there had never before been an evangelistic crusade of any kind for the Danes to attend.

1965—MONTGOMERY, ALABAMA

After the Hawaiian Crusade in early February (the telecast of which brought over 800,000 letters in one month to the Evangelistic Association) Billy Graham, heeding President Lyndon Johnson's personal advice, accepted an invitation to bring the Crusade to Montgomery's Crampton Bowl—so long as the audience was not segregated. In every audience in this Alabama crusade at least one-third were Negroes, sitting wherever they liked, and the choir was half Negro half white, entirely integrated.

1965—HOUSTON, TEXAS

Following Montgomery, there were crusades in Vancouver, B. C., Seattle and Denver before the Team went to Houston. The second crusade held in Houston, was in the space-age Astrodome, the largest enclosed stadium in the world. It was the first crusade ever attended by a President of the United States: Lyndon Baines Johnson.

1966—GREENVILLE, SOUTH CAROLINA

In the spring of 1966 Billy Graham and the Team brought the crusade to Textile Hall in Greenville, South Carolina. Dr. Graham had had a serious operation in the fall of 1965, and had returned to the hospital due to recuperative complications.

When the Greenville Crusade opened, he still had not regained his full strength, but when it became evident that the 20,000 seats of the Textile Hall could not begin to hold the crowds, for the first time anywhere the crusade was held twice daily, in the afternoon and at night. This crusade was notable for concentrating on youth, and the problems of youth; and the youth of South Carolina responded in record number both in attendance and in coming forward to make decisions.

1966—GREATER LONDON

In June of 1966 began one of the most troubling crusades of Billy Graham's life—the second Greater London Crusade. London, beset with economic difficulties and political uncertainties, had become the City of the Mods and the Rockers, mini-skirts and Beatlemania—apparently a city gone mad in comparison to the staid London of the past. Earl's Court, the largest indoor arena in London, was adapted to hold 23,000 people and for the first time closed circuit television made it possible to bring the crusade live to any city in England.

As one London newsman said: "Ours is an old country, and many and many famous personages have visited these shores—but no one man in our long and illustrious history has ever been able to both enthrall and upset an entire nation as Billy Graham has done in England in the year 1966."

*   *   *   *   *

In the seventeen years since the first crusade in the canvas tent in Los Angeles, through the Greater London Crusade more than one million persons by actual count have "come forward" at Billy Graham Crusades to make their decision for Christ. The number of people that have been brought to faith through the Billy Graham films, television and radio is of course inestimable.

Biographical Sketch

WILLIAM (BILLY) F. GRAHAM
Founder and President
Billy Graham Evangelistic Association

BORN	November 7, 1918	
	Charlotte, North Carolina	
PARENTS	William Franklin (deceased, 1962) and Morrow Coffey Graham	
MARRIED	Ruth McCue Bell, 1943	
EDUCATION	1940	B.Th., Florida Bible Institute, Tampa, Florida
	1943	B.A., Wheaton College, Wheaton, Illinois
VOCATION	1940	Ordained in Southern Baptist Church
	1943–45	Pastor, First Church, Western Springs, Illinois Radio personality, "Song in the Night," on station WCFL, Chicago, Illinois
	1946	First Vice-President, Youth for Christ International. Began Crusade for Christ

	1947–51	President, Northwestern Schools (now Northwestern College), Minneapolis, Minnesota
	1950–	Founder of weekly "Hour of Decision" radio program; now on more than 1,000 stations
		Founded Billy Graham Evangelistic Association, Minneapolis, Minnesota

PUBLISHED
WORKS

	1953	"Peace With God"
	1955	"The Secret of Happiness"
	1960	"My Answer"
	1965	"World Aflame"

Author of syndicated newspaper column, "My Answer," carried by 132 daily newspapers

MAJOR
CRUSADES

Major evangelistic crusades in almost every state in the United States, and in more than 60 foreign countries

HONORARY
DEGREES

Dr. Graham holds honorary degrees from more than twenty colleges and universities

AWARDS
AND
HONORS

Fellow of Royal Geographic Society
Member of Royal Literary Society
Freedoms Foundation Distinguished Persons Award, 1955
"Clergyman-Churchman of the Year" by the Washington Pilgrimage, 1956

Gold Medal Award, National Institute of Social Science, N. Y., 1957

"Mr. Applause" of 1957

Most Photographed Man in America Award, Sylvania Corp., 1957

Salesman of the Year, Sales Executive Club of New York, 1958

Ninth International Youth's Distinguished Service Citation, 1961

Bernard Baruch Award of the Veterans of Foreign Wars, for contribution to world peace, 1955

Annual Gutenberg Award of the Chicago Bible Society, 1962

Gold Award of the George Washington Carver Memorial Institute, for contribution to race relations, 1963

The UPPER ROOM Citation for "Man of the Year in Religion," 1964

Clergyman of the Year, National Pilgrim Society

Distinguished Service Medal of the Salvation Army

Speaker of the Year Award, 1964

Golden Plate Award, American Academy of Achievement, 1965

Gallup Poll "Religious Man of the Year" for five consecutive years

Horatio Alger Award, 1965

Who's Who, annually since 1954

Appears regularly on list of "Ten Most Admired Men in the World" of The Gallup Poll 1951–1966

National Citizenship Award by the Military

Chaplains Association of the U.S.A., 1965

Big Brother of the Year Award at the White House, Washington, D. C., 1966 for contribution to the welfare of children

CHILDREN Virginia Leftwich (Mrs. Stephan Tchividjian), 1945

Anne Morrow (Mrs. Danny Lotz), 1948

Ruth Bell, 1950

William Franklin, Jr., 1952

Nelson Edman, 1958

RESIDENCE Montreat, North Carolina

OFFICES Minneapolis, Minnesota

Atlanta, Georgia

New York City, New York

Burbank, California (World Wide Pictures)

Winnipeg, Canada

London, England

Paris, France

Frankfurt, Germany

Sydney, Australia

Buenos Aires, Argentina

Honolulu, Hawaii (radio station KAIM)

Black Mountain, N. C. (radio stations WFGW-AM and WMIT-FM)